Mike Miller, currently a student at Harvard University, was the youngest person (when he was thirteen) to have a crossword puzzle published in *The New York Times*. Since then, he has taught two courses in crossword puzzles at the New School for Social Research in New York City, and articles about him have appeared in *The New York Times, The New Yorker,* the *Chicago Tribune,* and the major wire services.

Mike Miller

beyond crossword puzzles

Prentice-Hall, Inc., Englewood Cliffs, New Jersey 07632

Library of Congress Cataloging in Publication Data

Miller, Mike (date)
  Beyond crossword puzzles.
  1. Word games.   2. Crossword puzzles.   I. Title.
GV1507.W8M54   1983   793.73   83-3326

10 9 8 7 6 5 4 3 2

Editorial/production supervision
and interior design by Kimberly Mazur
Cover design © 1983 Jeannette Jacobs
Manufacturing buyer: Pat Mahoney

Prentice-Hall International, Inc., *London*
Prentice-Hall of Australia Pty. Limited, *Sydney*
Prentice-Hall Canada Inc., *Toronto*
Prentice-Hall of India Private Limited, *New Delhi*
Prentice-Hall of Japan, Inc., *Tokyo*
Prentice-Hall of Southeast Asia Pte. Ltd., *Singapore*
Whitehall Books Limited, Wellington, *New Zealand*
Editora Prentice-Hall do Brasil Ltda., *Rio de Janeiro*

contents

Preface

If you are a crossword puzzle fan and have never tried solving anything other than the conventional crossword in your daily newspaper, you have been eating TV dinners all your life while a world of four-star French restaurants lies waiting for you. This book is your guide to that world.

At first glance, for someone good at newspaper crosswords but weary of them and ready to move on, there doesn't seem to be anywhere to turn. Those puzzles without diagrams on the bottom of the Sunday *Times* puzzle page look impossible. As for the misshapen "cryptic" crosswords that appear in the *Times* every so often, and in the back of *Harper's, The Atlantic, The Nation,* and *New York,* the *clues* don't even seem to make sense.

I can sympathize with the plight of such a solver because I was once one myself—until I learned how to solve those mysterious crossword variants. The new puzzles were a revelation to me: the faint buzz of satisfaction that came with completing my daily four-fifths of a *Times* puzzle before the *amahs* and the *Omoos* stumped me was easily surpassed by the thrill of piecing together a single chunk of a diagramless puzzle, of solving a single cryptic clue.

It is not hard to account for the pleasure these puzzles can give. Whereas ordinary crossword puzzles depend entirely on the accumulation of obscure knowledge, diagramlesses and cryptics are real *puzzles*—they depend on wit and logic. Their format is the same as a crossword puzzle's—the endlessly appealing gimmick of solving definitions for interlocking words—but their content is far more devious and sophisticated.

About the time I discovered cryptics and diagramlesses, I began to try my hand at constructing puzzles—double crostics as well as crosswords. This, too, I found a more satisfying pastime than solving conventional crosswords.

What struck me most about these new crossword puzzle adventures was that they had all been so simple to learn. Becoming good at diagramlesses and cryptics is completely different from becoming good at ordinary crosswords. No one really *learns* how to do a newspaper crossword puzzle—there's nothing to teach. No conventional crossword in the world comes with a set of instructions.

The puzzles I was now solving needed a set of instructions— that was all. Learning how to solve cryptics and diagramlesses and construct crosswords and double crostics, I discovered, was just a matter of following a new set of rules and strategies. A competent crossword fan only needs someone to explain the new rules for his puzzle horizons to be instantly expanded.

That's what I intend to do here: explain these new instructions to word-game fans who are ready to go beyond crossword puzzles.

This book grew out of a course in advanced crosswords I taught twice at the New School for Social Research in New York. In gathering material for the course, I accumulated a great many anecdotes and legends about the history of crosswords and other word games, and I have sprinkled these throughout the book. The first anecdote—the introduction that follows this preface—tells the story of the unusual four months I spent in 1977, teaching a dozen adults at the New School. It was not merely the curriculum that was unusual: The youngest student in the class was 22, and that made him exactly eight years older than I.

ACKNOWLEDGMENTS

I am grateful to Harriet Wilson and Will Weng for helping me track down several puzzles. My debt to Roger Millington's *Crossword Puzzles: Their History and Their Cult* and Dmitri A. Borgmann's *Language on Vacation* is sizable; I have cited these two excellent books throughout the text.

I must also thank Oscar Collier, the editor who first conceived this book; Anne Malcolm of the Lymond Institute, whose research in logodaedaly proved invaluable; and Steven Miller, my able secretary and treasurer.

Finally, for their encouragement and editorial advice, I thank my mother and father, who taught me every word game in this book; and Sarah Paul, who has been my best guide to the world beyond crossword puzzles.

The excerpts from Dmitri A. Borgman, *Language on Vacation* © 1965 Dmitri A. Borgman (New York: Charles Scribner's Sons, 1965). Reprinted with the permission of Charles Scribner's Sons.

The excerpt on page 34 is from *The Brand New Monty Python Papperbok*, by Graham Chapman, John Cleese, Terry Gilliam, Eric Idle, Terry Jones, and Michael Palin, and published by Eyre Methuen. Reprinted with permission of Python Productions.

The excerpt from *Night Thoughts* by Edmund Wilson © 1953, 1961 by Edmund Wilson. Used by permission of Farrar, Straus, and Giroux, Inc.

The puzzles entitled "Theme and Variations," "Noel," and "HI (Shorthand I)," and their solutions, by Emily Cox and Henry Rathvon, © 1979 by the Atlantic Monthly Company, Boston, Massachusetts. Reprinted by permission.

The puzzles entitled "New Directions," Winners First," "Viscious Circles II," and "Chessman" and their solutions are reprinted by permission from *Stephen Sondheim's Crossword Puzzles*, Harper & Row, 1980.

The puzzle entitled "Tossed Salad" and its solution, by

introduction

One afternoon in the fall of 1977, I skipped my last class at school and took the subway downtown to the New School for Social Research. Walking among the northern blocks of Greenwich Village, I arrived at the school's 12th Street entrance and rode the elevator up to the office of Dean Reuben Abel.

A small crowd had already formed a line outside the dean's office, all there—like I was—to propose a course for the school's spring catalogue. In front of me was a woman with a proposal for a seminar on Plato's cave. Behind me were two other women who hoped to team teach a course in cloisonné. They asked me what I was doing in line, and I told them that I was interested in teaching a course in advanced crossword puzzles, an idea that apparently amused them.

But if any institution in New York would consider offering a class in crossword puzzles, I thought, it was the New School. A university with a respected tradition of instruction in the social sciences, the New School features a variety of academic courses in all disciplines, granting undergraduate and graduate degrees. In addition, its curriculum is celebrated for a remarkably eclectic selection of unorthodox courses; a typical term's offerings include classes in tai-chi, bongo-drumming, moped mechanics, meat cutting, and self-awareness. All in all, the New School is best known as a place where adults come one night a week to take the courses they always wanted to take; in fact, one category in its catalogue is called just that: "Courses You Always Wanted to Take."

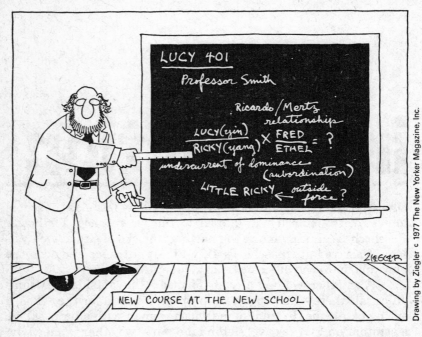

NEW COURSE AT THE NEW SCHOOL

When my turn came, Dean Abel called me into his office and I shook hands with him and told him my name. I had avoided revealing my age in the course proposal, since by way of biographical information I had simply written: "Aside from his proficiency at puzzle-solving and creating, Michael Miller is a devotee of palindromes, anagrams, pangrammatics, lipograms, and rhopalics." I am, in fact, a fan of anagrams and especially of palindromes—words and sentences that read the same way backwards and forward ("Draw putrid dirt upward.") But I was bluffing on the last three, which I had found in the index of a book of word games.

Dean Abel sat behind his desk and ruffled through a stack of papers until he found my proposal. I kept my eyes on him, expecting at any moment to see him shake his head, or at least lift an eyebrow, but his face remained completely straight.

"Tell me, Mr. Miller," he began. "What is your occupation?"

"I'm a student," I said carefully.

He nodded. "I see," he said. "And what do you study?"

At the time, I was studying math, English, chemistry, French, and Latin, and I debated whether to tell this to the Dean. "Well," I said finally, "I'm in high school."

He nodded soberly. "And what are your qualifications for teaching this course?" he asked.

I explained to him that learning advanced crosswords was just a matter of learning a new set of instructions and that anyone who already knew the instructions was perfectly qualified to pass them along.

After a few procedural questions about the course—how long did I think it would be, what nights could I teach it—the interview sounded like it was drawing to a close.

"Oh, one more question," said Dean Abel suddenly, looking at something on his desk. "What are rhopalics?"

I was lucky; I had come across the word purely by chance, only the night before. (I still had no idea what pangrammatics or lipograms were, though I do today: a pangrammatic is a sentence like "Pack my box with seven dozen jugs of liquor" that uses all twenty-six letters of the alphabet. A lipogram is a sentence, paragraph, or longer passage that avoids using a specified letter.)

A rhopalic, I told him, is a sentence in which each word has one letter more than the previous word, from the Greek word for "snowball."

I have never seen an expression of such patent disbelief as the look on Dean Abel's face as he ushered me out of the door, told me my proposal was "intriguing," and promised to get back to me.

In October, I received a form letter from the New School, notifying me that "Beyond Crossword Puzzles," as I had decided to call the course, had been accepted and was scheduled for four-teen hour-and-a-half sessions. The letter also mentioned that the course would have to be cancelled if less than twelve people enrolled in it.

With the letter came a brochure called "Teaching at the New School," which described the various advantages the New School's flexibility and diversity afforded an instructor. I was surprised to find that several of them applied to my own course:

> Many faculty members find a considerable satisfaction in ... the opportunity to work out an intellectual problem in the context of a fairly sophisticated dialectic, or in testing the viability of the solution to such an intellectual problem.

A few week laters, I received the catalogue. "Beyond Crossword Puzzles" was listed in the section entitled "Courses You Always Wanted to Take," between a course on casino gambling and a course called "The Art of Practical Joking." At the back of the catalog were brief biographies of all the instructors for the spring term. Most of them boasted several advanced degrees, and the two that did not even list a B.A. were quite conspicuous: one was a belly-dancer named Moon Rhythm and the other was me.

In planning the course, I wrote to five crossword puzzle celebrities, inviting them to appear as guest lecturers in my class. The first letter went to Margaret Farrar. Mrs. Farrar has been, without a doubt, the greatest single influence on the development of crosswords, and her career consists of a long string of firsts. As Margaret Petherbridge, she edited the *New York World*'s Sunday puzzles, the first crosswords ever to be printed. In 1924, two fledging publishers named Simon and Schuster asked her and two colleagues to edit a full book of crossword puzzles—the first such volume to be compiled. The book was an instant best-seller, establishing crosswords as a national mania, and today Mrs. Farrar (she married the publisher John Farrar in 1926) continues to edit Simon and Schuster's series of crossword books.

In 1942, the *New York Times*, which had been the only major newspaper in the country that didn't include crossword puzzles, capitulated to the craze and hired Mrs. Farrar to be the first *Times* puzzle editor, a post she held until her retirement in

1969. In short, Mrs. Farrar's life has *been* the history of crossword puzzles; there are still solvers who refer to their daily bout with the morning puzzle as "spending a little time with Margaret." Mrs. Farrar graciously agreed to speak to the class.

I also wrote to Will Weng, Mrs. Farrar's successor at the *Times*. He too accepted the invitation. "But don't count on me for any advice on the cryptic puzzles," he wrote. "They drive me crazy and I can't stand them."

Next, I wrote to Mel Taub, who constructed the "Puns and Anagrams" puzzles that the Sunday *Times* puzzle page featured until Eugene T. Maleska, Mr. Weng's successor, replaced them with cryptic puzzles. Mr. Taub continues to be a regular constructor of cryptics. "You might as well know I'm 15 years old," I told him, as I had Mrs. Farrar and Mr. Weng.

"You might as well know I'm three times your age," he wrote back. "It would be an honor to speak to your class, even though I can't imagine there could be anything beyond crossword puzzles."

The next letter went to Richard Maltby, Jr., the constructor of a fiendishly difficult series of cryptic puzzles for *New York* Magazine, and then for *Harper's*. He would have to decline my invitation, he replied, because he was directing a show about to open on Broadway—*Ain't Misbehavin'*.

Finally, I wrote to the composer and lyricist Stephen Sondheim, Mr. Maltby's predecessor at *New York* Magazine. Among cryptic fans, Mr. Sondheim's puzzles are legendary for their endless layers of complexity and deceit. "Thanks for the invitation," he wrote back, "but I'm afraid crossword puzzles are strictly a hobby of mine and I don't have much of interest to say."

He added, "Let me wish you good luck, however, with a venture that must surely be unique, not to mention bizarre."

In January, a month before "Beyond Crossword Puzzles" was scheduled to start, the course was written up in the *New York Times* and the Associated Press, and I began to receive a curious assortment of mail. Some correspondents poured out their complaints about crossword puzzles to me. "Dear Mike," wrote one, "Perhaps you can do something about this. So many times when a creator wants a 3-letter word, he will use ELA for the 6th degree of Guido's music scale. In any music history book you will consult, the 6th degree of Guido's scale is LA. . . . *Do something—please.*"

Others were interested to read that I was a palindrome enthusiast. One letter I received read, in its entirety: "How about WON TON? NOT NOW."

Another writer addressed the same subject in more emotional terms.

> I was especially delighted to find that you and your family like palindromes, because a couple of months ago, I made up some palindromes that I feel are pretty good ones, but it is so difficult to find anybody to really appreciate them. I told them to my husband and my parents, and I got reactions that amounted to slightly more than "So big deal, where's the punchline?"

Her creations included such gems as "Semite Moses orders a red rosé sometimes," and "I, Ed, sung an Agnus Dei." ("Forgive Ed's grammar," she added.)

Ruth Herschon of Manhattan, who described herself as "slightly anile" sent me the following exercise, which I show anyone who asks me whether doing puzzles has improved my vocabulary:

> An esne sat under an acer. The ani were chirping in its rami and Ra was all aglow. Down the iter came a Ute carrying a sac containing a snee, an epee, and an etui. "Wherever did you get those beautiful things?" asked the esne. And the Ute replied, "I got them with an agio, down at the stoa."

The same day's mail contained a three-page, single-spaced letter describing one man's futile attempt to understand diagramlesses.

A dentist in Connecticut had other ideas when he wrote to me. "The article in the *New York Times* described you in such a way," he wrote, "that I couldn't help think of a young woman in Washington D.C. who could be an interesting correspondent. . . . She can be awesome with words." The letter closed, "Hope there is a meeting of minds."

In February, I took the subway downtown to the New School for the second time. A week earlier, on the day the course was scheduled to get the knife for underenrollment, it had attracted its twelfth student. As I rode to the first meeting of "Beyond Crossword Puzzles," two questions occupied me: How would I keep the class occupied for an hour and a half, and how would they react to my age?

Regarding the first question, I figured, from my own experience as a student, that we would all tell each other a bit about ourselves and exchange a few gripes and anecdotes about crossword puzzles. Then I would briefly describe the course and let the class out early.

But it seemed to me that the second question rendered the first one moot. The same nightmare kept running through my mind: Most of the people in the class would walk out on the spot, and those that stayed would shake their heads in disgust for the whole hour and a half, muttering, "One hundred and fifteen dollars. For a lousy kid."

I was wrong on both counts. All twelve students were sitting around a big table as I walked into the classroom, and evidently, most of them had heard about my age. There were four women and eight men, and they ranged in age from about twenty-five to seventy-five. Before I arrived, they had been quietly chatting, and some of them had been doing the morning crossword puzzle, of all things, but they put down their pencils and fell silent as I walked in.

"You must be Michael," one of them said as I took a seat. I was too nervous to answer, and I smiled nervously. They were all smiling back at me, waiting silently to hear how I would begin.

Before I could start, someone shouted from the back, "What should we call you? Professor?"

"Call me Mike," I said. Everyone laughed; the ice was broken. Trying very hard not to sound like a teacher, I kept talking: "Why don't you each tell us your name and a little bit about what you hope to do in this course."

After everyone had given this information all twelve looked up at me, waiting for my next move. Novice that I was, I had started the class about five minutes early. I had a full hour and a half to fill

Fortunately, I had brought along a few puzzles and exercises to do. I had actually planned to use them in the second class, or even the third, figuring that the introductions and anecdotes might spill over into the second session. By the time I ended the class—early—we had gone through a long worksheet on anagrams, I had explained how to start attacking a diagramless, and we were about a quarter of the way through solving one.

From then on, I came to class prepared, with an ample stockpile of cryptics and diagramlesses to fill up any leftover time at the end of a session. Once, though, I was caught short. It was a dilemma I imagine most teachers have faced. The class was working through a diagramless puzzle, and three students were clearly much better at it than any of the others. In case the rest of the class hadn't realized this, the three were calling out all of the answers and periodically announcing that the puzzle was easy. Soon, I ran out of polite ways to ask them to shut up, so I let them set the pace for a while. And before long, it was clear that the other nine were completely lost. In this manner, I juggled the tempo of the class, alternately pleasing the three experts and then the other nine students, until the session was over.

The next week, I dug up an old Stephen Sondheim puzzle that I had been unable to complete. The puzzle was difficult even by Sondheim's standards; I quote from its instructions:

> The puzzle's words are formed by inserting three- or four-letter words in the five vertical columns formed by the sides of the diagram and the four columns of printed letters; except when marked X, these short words run from left to right. They are clued by two definitions: one word (A) from which another word (B) is subtracted; either the required word or (B) occurs unbroken in (A).

Before the next class started, I handed a copy of the puzzle to each of the three diagramless aces and suggested that they sit in the back of the classroom and see how they fared with it. The nine others and I proceeded to work through a difficult diagramless puzzle at a comfortable pace. For the rest of the session, the only sound that came from the back of the room was an occasional soft cry of triumph; when the class was over, the three aces presented me with three copies of the puzzle, completely solved. "Decent puzzle," one of them said as he walked out of the classroom.

The course's progress was punctuated by the appearance of several visitors. The first visit came from Dean Abel, who appeared at the first session and sat quietly in the back of the room for about a half hour, his straight face breaking into a slight smile only as he snuck out of the classroom.

Toward the middle of the course, the guest lecturers started arriving: Margaret Farrar, Will Weng, and Mel Taub. Their appearances proved to be among the course's high points, as they discoursed at great length upon the history of the crossword puzzle, the art of puzzle construction, and the work of a puzzle editor. After the last of them had appeared, one student in the class told me, "I never thought those names on the top of the puzzles were real. I still don't believe it—that they do crossword puzzles for a living."

The night of Mel Taub's appearance, the class had another visitor: my mother. I had established an easy rapport with the class at this point, but I still was uncomfortable with the prospect of her visit; it just seemed undignified to introduce my twelve students to their teacher's mom. So when she walked in, I casually told the class that she was my Aunt Janet, and no one gave it another thought.

I almost pulled it off without a hitch. Halfway through the session, when the entire class was stumped by a cryptic clue, I blurted out, "How about you, Mom?" The whole class looked up and I quickly muttered something about the old family resemblance and proceeded as if nothing had happened. A few members of the class gave Aunt Janet a suspicious looking over as the class continued, but no one ever called my bluff. In fact, I know there was at least one student who bought my story wholeheartedly. At the end of the class, he winked at my mother and offered her a ride home, and the following week, he kept remarking to me about what a charming aunt I had.

There was one other visitor who appeared with astonishing frequency, although none of us ever learned his name. One of the students in the class was Stanley H. Kaplan, the founder and eponymous czar of a successful chain of "educational centers" that offer preparatory courses for various standardized tests. Throughout the course, Mr. Kaplan was traveling around the country, visiting his centers and opening up new ones. Each time he missed the class—and he missed about half of them—a mysterious man would appear and set up a portable tape recorder, which he quietly reclaimed at the end of the hour and a half. By his third or fourth appearance, he no longer bothered to explain his mission, and pretty soon, his face was as familiar as any other student's; we would all greet him like an old friend and ask him where Stanley was that week.

At the fourteenth and final meeting of "Beyond Crossword Puzzles," we had finished covering the course's three topics—diagramlesses, cryptics, and puzzle construction—and so we had a small party. At the same time, I had not yet reached the legal drinking age in New York, but a couple of students brought in some wine and beer, and a few others arrived with cheese and bread. Two members of the class passed around puzzles they had just finished constructing, and a woman in the class who worked in publishing had copies of the *Dell Crossword Dictionary* for everyone. Mr. Kaplan was in town that day, and in the middle of the festivities, he pulled me aside and told me to look him up if I ever needed a job. Which I did, three years later.

My contribution to the party was a chocolate-cherry cake, with the following message inscribed in icing:

Farewell to muddle synthesis of ego and body (7)

The icer at the bakery had given me a dubious stare when I told her what to write, but it was a message the entire class understood instantly. And when you have read this book, which contains all the material covered in the course "Beyond Crossword Puzzles," you will understand the message too.

1
cryptic
puzzles

Before you read this chapter, try solving Crossword Puzzle #1. Notice that this puzzle differs from conventional crosswords in two simple respects. First, it contains unkeyed letters—letters that are not part of both an across-word and a down-word. In addition, after each definition, there is an extra hint in parentheses.

Puzzle 1

(Note: in the subsidiary definitions within parentheses, quotation marks indicate *definitions* of smaller words; capital letters indicate the *words* themselves.)

ACROSS

1.	Journalist David	(2 parts: "actor Holbrook"; anagram of BEST RAM)
6.	Batter's ploy	("obtuse" with "Roman 50" missing)
8.	Type of greens	(sounds like "nabbed")
9.	Lawn device	(3 parts: "Spanish, abbr."; "skating locale"; "Shakespearean king" with "article" missing)
11.	Linger aimlessly	(last two-thirds of "slave-laborer")
13.	Inventor Whitney	(middle letters of "keepsake")
14.	Alpine dwelling	("French article" inside "French cat")
15.	Beethoven piano work	(3 parts: "Napoleon, for one"; "agreement"; "zero")
19.	Bucolic	(2 parts: "iron corrosion"; "Roman 99")
21.	High rock	("decay" backwards)

22. Musical key   ("hush!" inside "freshwater fish")
24. Most prominent position   (anagram of ROT OF FERN)
26. Pasta casings   (hidden in OPERA VIOLINISTS)
27. Apprehends   (anagram of BANS)
28. Feigning   (pun: might be a shepherd's preliminary activity?)

DOWN

1. Twain protagonist   (2 parts: "blackish fruit"; "Scandinavian native")
2. Stick candy   ("tablet" backwards inside "circular path")
3. Escape, as arrest   ("commercial, for short" inside "Adam's wife")
4. Lather   ("potatoes" with "soft, musically" missing)
5. Lunatic   (2 parts: "mother, for short"; "Abel's murderer" backwards)
6. Library furniture   (anagram of OBOE SACK)
7. Stravinsky opus   (2 parts: sounds like "the conservative faction"; "progeny" with "loud, musically" missing)
10. New Jersey university   (2 parts: "royal son"; "2000 pounds")
12. Splitsville   ("lulu" backwards)
16. Ends of the spectrum   (anagram of MEETS REX)
17. Certain G-Man   (2 parts: "compass pt."; "circle section")
18. Ribbed macaroni   (2 parts: "Latvian capital"; "novelist Morrison")
20. Drive-in waiter   (hidden in OSCAR HOPES)
23. Brides and brothers number   (hidden in THESE VENDERS)
25. Turkey or fox   ("legal wrong" backwards)

We will discuss this puzzle later in this chapter, a chapter about the world's most enigmatic, intriguing, and addictive crossword—the cryptic puzzle.

For American puzzle fans, cryptics are available in several publications: *The Nation, Atlantic Monthly,* and *Harper's* publish one in the back of every issue; the *Sunday New York Times* sporadically replaces its monthly "Puns and Anagrams" puzzle with a cryptic; and *New York* regularly reprints the *Sunday Times of London*'s crossword, a cryptic that is billed presumptuously as "The World's Most Challenging Crossword."

In addition, a cryptic puzzle appears regularly in many of the newspapers and magazines of its country of origin—England. British crossword fans tend to treat the cryptic as a national treasure, and some get quite impassioned on the subject. In March of 1972, W. H. Auden, who was preparing to move from New York City to Oxford, wrote a short article for the Op-Ed page of the *New York Times* on the pleasures of living in New York:

> People ask me if I shall miss the "cultural life" here. My answer: I have never taken part in it. Since I like to go to bed very early, I seldom go to the theater or movies or concerts. My cultural life is confined to reading, listening to records of classical music, and solving crossword puzzles, activities I can indulge in anywhere. At this point, I must say that the crossword in *The New York Times* frequently drives me up the wall with rage because of the lack of precision in its clues. Time and again, one sees from the letters one has what the word must be, but the clue is inaccurate. The clues in British crosswords may be more complicated, but they are always fair. E.g., *Song goes dry for a ruined Dean.* Answer: *Serenade.*

To most American readers, Auden's example of a "fair" clue was, to say the least, cryptic. To anyone familiar with the structure and language of cryptic clues, however, it made perfect sense.

Now for a surprise: the clues in the puzzle you solved at the beginning of this chapter are, in simplified form, cryptic clues. Like that puzzle's clues, all cryptic clues consist of two discrete elements that indicate the solution in two separate ways.

One part is simply a *straight definition*, the sort of definition that would appear in a conventional American crossword puzzle; this part describes the *meaning* of the final solution.

The second part describes the solution using some sort of *wordplay*—for instance rearranging its letters or spelling it backward. (As you will discover, there are exactly eight types of wordplay at a cryptic cluemaker's disposal.)

The important thing to remember about the second part of a cryptic clue is that it has absolutely nothing to do with the final answer's *meaning*; it treats the solution only as a string of letters. This is the great leap you must make in order to solve a cryptic clue: you have to think of a word not only as a symbol for a particular meaning, but also as an ordered set of letters of the alphabet. "Tight end," you will learn, is not just a football position; it also indicates the letter *t* (that is, the end of the word *tight*).

What makes a cryptic clue so elegant and pleasing—and at the same time so infuriatingly inaccessible to solvers of conventional crosswords—is that its two elements are seamlessly blended intc one contiguous phrase or sentence (unlike the clues in the puzzle at the start of this chapter).

To the uninitiate, this final sentence tends to sound as meaningless and puzzling as "Song goes dry for a ruined Dean." A cryptic solver, however, learns to disregard the meaning of the full sentence and consider it as two discrete elements: the straight definition and the wordplay.

In return for the complex labors of dissecting cryptic clues, the solver has a treat: there are virtually no obscure "crossword-words" in cryptic puzzles. In the rare cases when a constructor must resort to an obscure word, you'll often be alerted to it, and possibly even given a hint about it. But in general, you can forget all you know about blue dyes and seed-cases and Oriental nurse-maids—you won't need them. All you'll need to know to solve a cryptic crossword is the eight types of cryptic wordplay.

1. DOUBLE DEFINITIONS

In a well-made cryptic clue, the two basic elements are contiguous; you can draw a line between two words in the clue and the straight definition will lie on one side and the wordplay on the other, leaving no extraneous words.

This fact leads to the first important strategy to remember in solving a cryptic crossword: look for the straight definition at either end of the clue. It will usually be the first few words or the last few words.

The simplest application of this strategy comes in the simplest type of cryptic clue: the double definition. In a double-definition clue, two different meanings of the same word are juxtaposed in a misleading way. The wordplay part of the clue, in other words, is just another straight definition. Here's an example:

Many entertainers (5).

(Note: after each clue, the number of letters in the solution is given, to save you the trouble of counting up the squares.)

To solve this clue, pay no attention to the meaning of the *full* definition; forget that in a conventional puzzle, this clue might mean something like *troupe* or *chorus*. This is exactly what the cluemaker is trying to lure you into thinking. Instead, break the clue into its two components, and try to find a word that means both "many" and "entertainers."

As you may have already guessed, the answer here is *hosts*.

A breed of double-definition clue that crops up from time to time is one in which a phrase's literal and figurative meanings are both defined. For example:

Punch the bag and go to bed (3, 3, 4).

(The numbers in parentheses indicate that the answer will have three words—two of three letters and one of four.) The answer to this one is *hit the sack*.

As you will see, certain clues contain indicators—words that serve as instructions for disentangling the wordplay part of the clues. These indicators are also useful as a way to determine the *type* of wordplay involved in a given clue. Double definitions do not contain indicators, but there is still a good way to sniff them out: look for them in very short clues. In general, in a clue of just two or three words; a double definition is the only type of wordplay simple enough for the clue to contain.

Here are a few more double-definition clues for you to try. (In these clues, you're working under a disadvantage, since you don't have crossing words to give you letters. On the other hand, you have the decided advantage of knowing exactly what type of clue you're up against.) Worksheet answers begin on page 145.

DOUBLE DEFINITION WORKSHEET

1. Suit golfer's needs (5)
2. Somber burial place (5)
3. Vitally important bird (8)
4. Pulverized the earth (6)
5. State rapid transit (7)

2. HIDDEN WORDS

Often, phrases and sentences conceal consecutive letters that spell out full words. In the previous sentence, for instance, the words *sands, sconce, hats,* and *lout* are hidden.

This is the principle of the hidden word clue: the wordplay part of the clue contains—either within a single word or spread out across several—the letters of the solution, in order. For example:

There's integrity in each one's tyranny (7).

The solution: *honesty.* "Integrity" is the straight definition and the answer is lurking in "each one's tyranny."

This clue, like nearly all hidden word clues, contains an indicator—a signal to look for a hidden word. In this case, the indicator is simply the word "in." The word is not strictly part of the straight definition and not part of the hidden word; its function in the clue is to tell you that the solution is hidden *in* "each one's tyranny."

Of course not every clue containing the word *in* is necessarily a hidden word clue, but every hidden word clue *does* contain the word, or a suitable equivalent. Words such as *within, holds, containing,* and *at the heart of* are other common indicators for a hidden word clue.

In addition, this clue illustrates a basic rule of cryptic clue solving, one that is printed in the instructions of many cryptic puzzles: *ignore punctuation.* Here, the apostrophe in *one's* happens to land in the middle of the hidden answer; disregard it. If you come across an ampersand, a dollar sign, a parenthesis, a quotation mark—anything, in short, that is not an actual letter—ignore it.

One final note about hidden word clues: sometimes, the solution will be hidden backward, from right to left. This twist will always be indicated in the clue. For example:

Slightly back in style to merchants (8).

The answer: *remotely* (straight definition: "slightly"), which lies *back in* (that is, *backward within*) "style to merchants."

Hidden word clues are the most fun when you aren't expecting them— when the answer pops out at you all of a sudden—but here are a few more examples to try.

HIDDEN WORD WORKSHEET
1. Revel in rubbing elbows (5)
2. Urban anarchist bears fruit (6)
3. Traditional legend back in mighty Mesopotamia (4)
4. Hint: I'm a tease to hold a close friend (8)
5. Mutt is inside, among relatives (7)

The clues in this puzzle are all of the two types we've covered so far. If you need a hint, turn to page 62 to find out which clue is which type.

Puzzle 2

ACROSS

1. Bringing to a higher court and winning (9)
6. Opening may fill with wonder (8)
9. Worked in a darkroom and gradually matured (9)
11. Having a good deal of experience spiced up (8)
14. Judicial pronouncements—they're ungrammatical when they run on (9)

DOWN

2. Chessman's musical composition (5)
3. Bearing melody (3)
4. Precipitation concludes with particle (3)
5. Avarice within Legree disappears (5)
7. Adolescence, in haste, ensues (5)
8. Oak nut in a cornfield (5)
9. Sprinkles powder and wipes it away (5)
10. Restricted diet holds cantor (5)
12. Hoofer Miller's cape (3)
13. Somebody's unit (3)

3. HOMOPHONES

Two words are homophones if they sound alike but are spelled differently. A homophone clue is one in which a word and its homophone are both defined. The indicator in this sort of clue is easy to spot. Here's an example:

> Sounds like M. Monet's scratched (6).

This clue is telling you to find a word for "scratched" that sounds like a word defined by "M. Monet." The answer: *clawed*, a homophone for *Claude*.

The indicator in a homophone clue may be more oblique than this one. Words such as *hear, spoken, aloud,* and *oral* should all alert you to a homophone clue.

Sometimes a homophone clue will involve several words. For instance:

> Greek water resounds with a G in a different key (6, 3).

The answer: *Aegean Sea,* a homophone for *a G in C*.

HOMOPHONE WORKSHEET
1. State most important sounds (5)
2. Hear prohibited musicians (4)
3. Slaps increase, we hear (6)
4. Baker listens to soft whispering noise (7)
5. An explosive in a male elephant sounds loathsome (10)

The clues in the following puzzles are all of the three types we've covered so far. To find out which clue is which type, turn to the hints on page 63.

Puzzle 3

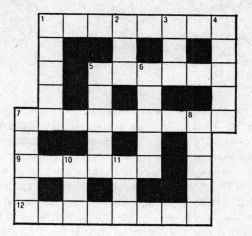

ACROSS

1. Reducing the speed of sound's shattering (8)
5. Gist of word I spell S-C-A-T-T-E-R (6)
7. Dwellers dwelling loudly (9)
9. Sounds like the gambler's improved (6)
12. Direct, narrow waterway's noise (8)

DOWN

1. Intrepid Indian tribesman (5)
2. Boxer at the core of reality (3)
3. Little devil's inside him playfully (3)
4. Cheats sea birds (5)
5. Wander aimlessly—that's the general idea (5)
6. Sounds completely pure to clip a sheep's hair (5)
7. We're busy comprehending a picture puzzle (5)
8. Pursued out loud the political pamphlet (5)
10. Sailor's pitch (3)
11. Yale student sitting in Beinicke Library (3)

4. REVERSALS

Here's a typical reversal clue:

Repairman returns to make the sweater again (6)

You can probably figure out the cryptic way to read this clue: "return" a word for "repairman"—read it backward, in other words—to get the solution, a word meaning "to make the sweater again." The answer· *reknit*

This is the way all reversal clues work: the wordplay part of the clue defines the word formed by writing the solution backward. You will always see an indicator in this sort of clue—a word like *returns* that tells you that the solution is being reversed. Other indicators you are likely to encounter include *back, up* (for a down clue), *overturned,* and *the wrong way.*

Notice that there is an ambiguity in the way the above clue is worded—an ambiguity that many reversal clues contain. The straight definition could be "repairman" and the wordplay "returns to make the sweater again," in which case the solution would be *tinker*; or the straight definition could be "to make the sweater again" and the wordplay "repairman returns," in which case the solution would be *reknit.* In any reversal clue in which the indicator falls between the two definitions, you'll face a similar dilemma, and of course both possible solutions will always have the same number of letters. The only way to know for sure which is correct is to get a letter or two from crossing words.

Some more reversal clues to try:

REVERSAL WORKSHEET
1. Cauldron's lid is back (3)
2. Rodents may crawl up celebrity (4)
3. Find humor in overturning disaster (4)
4. Return infant's item to get reimbursed (6)
5. Exalted to the rank of God, either way you look at it (7)

Puzzle 4

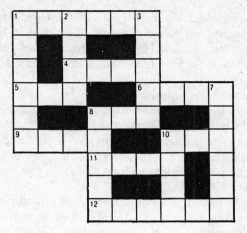

ACROSS

1. Charged for loud fashion (6)
4. Swarm back to make an acquaintance (4)
5. Frozen water may coat a pastry (3)
6. No palace contains this gem (4)
8. Noisy star's offspring (3)
9. Wicked to exist the wrong way (4)
10. Overthrown deity—Cerberus, for instance (3)
11. Formerly in prison cell (4)
12. Students back up error (6)

DOWN

1. Makes beer loudly to injure the ego (6)
2. Spoils sound for Renaissance instrument (4)
3. Runyon's an upset wanderer (5)
7. Illuminates lands (6)
8. Small puddles capsized the sailboat (5)
10. Sideline includes an informal cold-cuts shop (4)

5. WORD CHAINS

The word chain clue is the only cryptic clue that Marx is known to have thoroughly espoused. I refer, of course, to Harpo Marx. As movie fans will recall, Harpo communicated exclusively in elaborate charades; for instance, this is how he warns Chico of an impending bombshell:

Harpo makes exaggerated spooning motions with one hand and slurps from an imaginary bowl; soon Chico cries out "Soup!" Harpo takes a pair of imaginary chopsticks, chews vigorously, and shovels away into his mouth; Chico yells "Rice!" Harpo slurps, shovels, slurps, shovels: Chico yells "Soup, rice, soup, rice," and then finally "Surprise!" Harpo slaps Chico on the back and drops his left leg into Chico's arms.

This is essentially the way word chain clues work. The wordplay part consists of definitions of two or more words that, taken consecutively, spell out the solution. Here's an example:

Pelt markers can be fierce (7).

A pelt is a *fur*; markers are *IOU's*; put them together and they spell *furious*, meaning "fierce."
Here's another:

Am I capable or agreeable? (7)

The answer: *amiable* ("am I able?").
This clue illustrates two facts you should keep in mind about word chain clues. First, there can be more than two components involved in the wordplay; this clue has three. Second, the clue may contain a component itself, rather than its definition, as this clue contains "am" and "I."

WORDCHAIN WORKSHEET
1. Slim monarch is cogitating (8)
2. Be wary of vapor and oxidation (8)
3. Belonging to them, the tax collectors (6)
4. Annoying fellow is after two articles on a metrical foot (7)
5. Lookalike brother and little Edward are twisted together (6)

Puzzle 5

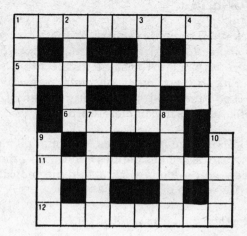

ACROSS

1. Chained up the cabin and showed the way (8)
5. Wager with Milland and Capone constitutes treason (8)
6. Meager bowling score (5)
11. Prickler and heavyweight make author wilder (8)
12. Agreeable insect at first appeals (8)

DOWN

1. U-Boats' heroes (3)
2. Part of recital to star certain female singers (5)
3. Hen's coating (5)
4. Printing sign to get rid of loud business transaction (4)
7. Paid athletes speaking unpoetic speech (5)
8. Additional contents of next ration (5)
9. Pace for teachers' favorites to rise (4)
10. Acrid taste returns to tiny insect (4)

6. CONTAINERS

What remarkable linguistic feature do these five words have in common: *comet, wallet, terrier, bothered,* and *startling*?

To begin with, notice that all five contain shorter words within them: *me, all, err, other,* and *tart,* respectively. And now look again: the letters that remain after the shorter words have been extracted also form complete words: *cot, wet, tier, bed,* and *sling.*

A container clue capitalizes on this phenomenon. The wordplay part of these clues defines two words—the outside word and the inside word—along with a suitable indicator. Here's an example that uses one of the above words:

Put everything in a moist billfold (6).

Pull *all* ("everything") in *wet* ("moist") and you get *wallet* ("billfold").

Another example:

Cookie's dream about a car (8).

This clue is noteworthy for three reasons. First, it uses the word *about* in a way that is devious but common in container clues; here the word's meaning is "on all sides of" or "surrounding."

Second, the "inside word" is actually two words. In general, either component of a container clue—the inside or the outside—may be more than one word.

Finally, one component appears in the clue undisguised, as opposed to being indicated by a definition—a common practice in container clues.

As you may have guessed, the solution to this clue is *macaroon: moon* ("dream" in its sense as a verb) is surrounding (that is, "about") *a car.*

The word *without,* meaning "the opposite of within," frequently appears in this kind of clue, serving the same function as *about* in the previous clue. Other common indicators for container clues include *around, outside, surrounding, enclosing,* and their synonyms; and words like *inside, within, amid,* and *at the heart of.*

A final note: beware of any word that begins with the prefix *in-*; chances are it's a concealed indication of a container clue. "Not indeed" means only one thing in a cryptic puzzle: *denoted.* "Favorite income" leads to *compete* and "All of us may be inbred" leads to *brewed.*

CONTAINER WORKSHEET

1. Am in a storage shack, humiliated (7)
2. Proposition: metal may be inside them (7)
3. Pursue, as in a Bolivian guerilla (5)
4. Buffalo receptacle—about so (5)
5. Principal man around me (4)

Puzzle 6

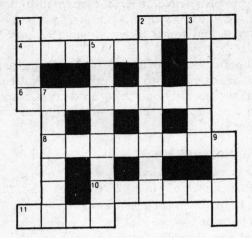

ACROSS

2. Syndicated adviser in Arab byroad (4)
4. Historian Edward's ape (6)
6. Perform song about summit-talking (8)
8. Communist "forests" trees (8)
10. Prep-school wallows in sex eternally (6)
11. Moistens ragout the wrong way (4)

DOWN

1. Grows older in historical time-periods (4)
2. Against departed daughter of Oedipus (8)
3. Implored for some breakfast in bed (6)
5. In certain cheeses and liqueurs (8)
7. Penzance denizen makes pastry without informer (6)
9. Fly high, sounding angry (4)

7. FRAGMENTS: BEHEADMENTS CURTAILMENTS, BORDERS, AND SUBTRACTIONS

In his remarkable book *Language on Vacation*, Dmitri A. Borgmann discusses the linguistic phenomena of beheadment and curtailment—apheresis and apocope, in the cant of wordplayers. By way of definition, here is Borgmann's example of an eight-stage beheadment:

> ASPIRATE
> SPIRATE
> PIRATE
> IRATE
> RATE
> ATE
> TE
> E

And here is an eight-stage curtailment, also from Borgmann:

> PASTERNS
> PASTERN
> PASTER
> PASTE
> PAST
> PAS
> PA
> P

It's not hard to see how a cryptic clue can make use of these two tricks: the wordplay part will define a word that, beheaded or curtailed by one letter, results in the solution. Here's a clue that uses one of the above examples:

Topless buccaneer is enraged (5).

A buccaneer is a *pirate*; "topless"—that is, without its first letter—it becomes *irate*, which the clues defines as "enraged." Other common indicators for this sort of clue, aside from *topless*, include *headless*, *beheaded*, and *decapitated*.

A curtailment clue works exactly the same way. For example:

Badger's almost unnecessary (7).

The answer: *needles* (the straight definition is "badgers") which is *needless* ("unnecessary") without its last letter. The curtailment is indicated by the word "almost."

It's worth noting a common cluemaker's ploy that appears in this clue. When one reads the complete clue, the word *badger* appears to be a noun. In its cryptic function as a straight definition, it's actually a verb. You'll encounter this sort of part-of-speech deception again and again.

Among the other indicators you're likely to find in a curtailment clue are *nearly, not quite, tailless,* and *bottomless*.

Here's a fragment clue of a different breed:

Base situated on village's outskirts (4).

The answer: *vile*, which is situated on the outskirts of the word vil–lag–e. The straight definition is "base." (This is another example of a word whose part of speech in the clue is misleading. "Base" serves as a noun in the clue; as a straight definition, it's an adjective.)

You'll be alerted to this sort of border clue by indicators such as *outlying, framing, surrounding,* and *at the edges*.

Finally, a fourth type of fragment clue involves subtracting one word from another to arrive at the solution. Such a clue may delete a word from the middle of a longer word (making it sort of a reverse container clue), or it may delete a word from either end of a longer word (making it a reverse word-chain clue). Look for words like *missing, without, minus,* or simply *no* to indicate a subtraction clue. Here's a tricky example:

British island fruit without leaves (3).

The answer: *Man*, as in the Isle of Man. As for the wordplay part—"fruit without leaves"—"fruit" is *mangoes* and "leaves" is *goes*.

FRAGMENT WORKSHEET
1. Kind of furniture for a racetrack building without a front (5)
2. Royal daughters, endless royal sons (7)
3. Tiger depicted on rug's borders (3)
4. Arrived for unfinished brooch (4)
5. Roll away from court for a legal examination (5)

Puzzle 7

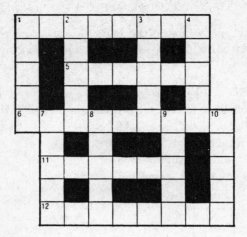

ACROSS

1. Author C.P. may let go of white flower (8)
5. Berliner is endlessly relevant (6)
6. Suffer intense longing about narrow piece of suit fabric (9)
11. In turn, I peel a vegetable (6)
12. Reenacted drama in tall grass (8)

DOWN

1. Pointed too high, musically (5)
2. Spleen for one church instrument (5)
3. Sounds like boarder's gossip (5)
4. Poster seen during Hopi nuptials (3-2)
7. Put in a grave dialogue with no opinion (5)
8. To make leather, strip back portions (5)
9. Hint, merely, with no beginning (5)
10. Over-imperiled, without rage (5)

8. ANAGRAMS

In the third century B.C., there lived a Greek poet by the name of Lycophron. Very little is known about his life and work; his only extant writings are a few fragments of a treatise on comedy. He is thought to have been a writer of tragedies, but none have survived. A dramatic monologue called "Alexandra"—a poem in 1474 iambic trimeters concerning Cassandra's prophecies during the Trojan War—is sometimes attributed to him, but not with any certainty.

But according to at least one source, in 260 B.C., Lycophron devised a monumental innovation that persists today in the unusual dual role of linguistic recreation and literary device: the anagram—a word or phrase that is a rearrangement of the letters of another word or phrase.

The anagram as wordplay is familiar enough: as a popular parlor game and, as we shall see, as a mainstay of cryptic crosswords. The anagram as literary device is somewhat less celebrated, but it has inspired the following:

- A full-sized collection of detective-story pastiches in which every proper name is an anagram—*The Anagram Detectives* by Norma Schier (The Mysterious Press, 1979). In one send-up of Sherlock Holmes, for instance, the detective's name is Hoskell Cholmers, his sidekick is named Sandwort, the two live on 221-A Krebb St.—you get the idea.

- At least one display of verbal pyrotechnics in the works of Vladimir Nabokov. The one I have in mind appears in *Lolita*. The nymphet of the title has been abducted, following a reckless automobile tour of the United States with her guardian and idolator, the novel's narrator Humbert Humbert, who has been having his way with his ward ever since a memorable night in a motel called the Enchanted Hunter. Lolita's abductor leaves Humbert a series of arcane clues to their whereabouts, in the form of entries in motel registers.

But the most penetrating bodkin was the anagramtailed entry in the register of Chestnut Lodge "Ted Hunter, Cane, NH."

- A comedy routine from the British troupe Monty Python's Flying Circus (from *The Brand New Monty Python Bok*):

Hello, and welcome to a page written entirely for people who dislike anagrams. Hi, anagram-haters everywhere! Down with all words or phrases formed with the letters of another! This page is specially dedicated to all who hate and despise the pathetic practice of shuffling letters to form different meanings. Let us make one thing clear from the start, there will be no anagrams on this page at all. None whatsoever. So anagram lovers can just turn to their own page, where they will find their pathetic practice sufficiently catered for. We want none of you here. For too long, we anti-anagrammatists have had to put up with the smugness of those meanings hidden in words or phrases. Now no more; this page is guaranteed free from anagrams. So just you put your feet up and relax without worrying whether you are reading concealed anagrams or not. Don't you just hate those bores who can crack an anagram faster than they can pour the irate? I'm sorry. That wasn't an anagram. It was a typing error. It was a printer's slip. The phrase "heat our tripe" should have read "I rape her tout." Oh golly. Sorry. I'm afraid that owing to a mistake in the proofreading, the phrase "rip her eat out" has been wrongly corrected to "ripe teat hour." On crikey. I'm terribly sorry but the phrase "our pi theatre" which we wrongly informed you was "the route pair" should have been printed "rather I toupe" and not "ripe hate tour." Oh no. Drat the bally thing. I'm most frightfully sorry but the phrase "Report the A.I.U." has been wrongly given as "therapeutior," when it should quite obviously have read "opiate hurter". . . .

It looks very much as though this page written especially for people who dislike anagrams has been sabotaged. It appears that someone has infiltrated the text at a crucial stage and tampered with the words, so that certain phrases have been red teal (7). We apologise to all haters of anagrams for the annoyance and inconvenience. Its all very ira tit gin r (1). But there you ear (3). What can neo od? (3-2) We are taking legal pests (5) to tup (3) the matter right but until then we can only loose a pig (9). The Tiredo (6).

Finally, even the simplest, isolated anagram can have its literary merit. In *Palindromes and Anagrams* (Dover Publications, 1973), Howard Bergerson has collected more than a thousand astonishing examples of anagrams that refer to their originals, including such wonders as:

desperation—a rope ends it
Ivanhoe by Sir Walter Scott—a novel by a Scottish writer
the nudist colony—no untidy clothes

Bergerson writes, "The attentive reader will discover in this abundance of examples, here given, of this diminutive art-form— even as he would were he studying some lovely Golden Treasury of Japanese haiku—moments of rare and incredibly delicate beauty."

With such an illustrious history, it is small wonder that the anagram is a crucial element of cryptic crossword puzzles. You can probably guess how an anagram clue works: the wordplay part of the clue is an anagram of the solution. Here's an example:

Wither terribly and twist in pain (6).

The answer: *writhe*, an anagram of "wither," defined as "twist in pain." Notice that the word "terribly" serves here as an indicator; it tells you to consider the word "wither" with its letters in the wrong order—spelled terribly, as it were. There are endless words a cluemaker may use to tip you off to an anagram; suffice it to say that the indicator in an anagram clue will always describe an unnatural or undesirable condition.

An anagram clue can involve an anagram of more than one word. For instance:

Brightness at night breaks up the thin gloom (9).

Here, the solution is an anagram of "thin gloom"; "breaks up" is the indicator, and "brightness at night" is the straight definition. The solution: *moonlight*.

This clue illustrates a good way to ferret out anagram clues: always be on the lookout for combinations of consecutive words in the clue that have the required number of letters. Here, for instance, "thin gloom" should jump out at you as potential grist for the anagram mill.

Sometimes, the words of the anagram will not be consecutive, but the cluemaker will be sure to indicate this. For instance:

It gets mixed with a noted remedy (8).

The wordplay part of this clue, repunctuated, reads "*It* gets mixed with *a noted*"; in other words, rearrange the letters ITA-NOTED. The answer is *antidote*, defined in the clue as "remedy."

Here's a corollary to the ferreting-out rule: look for unlikely words—especially proper nouns—that don't seem to make much sense in the clue. Chances are they're in there because they're felicitously spelled. For instance, if you see this clue:

Alf goes crazy with Walter's cascades (10).

It's a safe bet that Alf and Walter are not part of the straight definition. Sure enough, *Alf* and *Walter's* add up to ten letters; you can be sure they're an anagram for a word meaning "cascades."

Once you think you've spotted an anagram in a clue, there are several different ways to go about permuting the letters until you arrive at the solution. Some solvers find it helpful to write the letters in a circle, to let the eye fall on as many different combinations of letters as possible. Mel Taub, the *New York Times*'s top cryptic constructor, suggests writing the vowels on one line, the consonants on another—a trick that works surprisingly well.

A third way is to cross out common combinations of letters—such as ING, TION, or any full word contained with the diagram—and then work with the remaining letters. For instance, if you're trying to make a word out of the letters ALFWALTERS, you might notice the word *water*. Crossing it out leaves you with ALFLS, which is not difficult to unscramble into *falls*.

ANAGRAM WORKSHEET

1. Badly staple folds of cloth (6)
2. Coarse, misshapen scars (5)
3. Fellow player on lousy team (4)
4. Thelma misread Shakespeare's tragedy (6)
5. Kennedy, for one, gives mangled card to me (8)

Puzzle 8

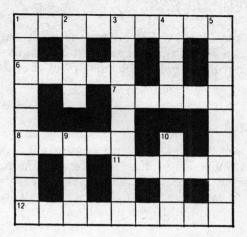

ACROSS

1. Psychiatrist for the sexual offender (9)
6. Secures boggy tracts of land (5)
7. Rapidly beat spoiled broth (5)
8. Bongo-drum bangs part for Cuban dance (5)
11. Inside, stumbling over the dialect (5)
12. Mafia don murders hated frog (9)

DOWN

1. Meddling with grip meant ruin (9)
2. Cupid's wound up (4)
3. Pacino's in Vienna's country and continent (9)
4. Stravinsky's uninitiated severity (4)
5. Piece of wood to buy for the way it sounds (3-2-4)
9. Lass amid turmoil (4)
10. Unit of measurement is 50% inchoate (4)

TWO RULEBREAKERS

These two types of clues are exceptions to the rule that every cryptic clue consists of two discrete parts: straight definition and wordplay. They occur only occasionally but they deserve a brief mention.

Double Duty

This is the perfect clue—the cryptic equivalent of one hand clapping. In a Double Duty clue, the straight definition and the wordplay are one and the same; the full clue serves both functions. This is, as you can guess, a difficult trick to pull off, so you won't encounter it very often. Here's an example.

A rope ends it tragically (11).

The answer is *desperation*, an anagram of "*a rope ends it*" (the anagram is indicated by "tragically"). In addition, the full clue is a straight definition of the solution.
Another example:

What may be read in these symposiums (6).

The solution is theses, which is hidden (that is, it may be read) in "these symposiums." Again, the full clue serves as a straight definition.

Horsing Around

Once in a while, a cluemaker will abandon all the rigors of cryptic crosswords and let loose with a pure, unabashed pun. This kind of clue will invariably be indicated by a question mark or an exclamation point. One example will give you the idea (this one comes from Richard Maltby):

Kind of sentence delivered by a hung jury? (9)

The answer: *suspended*.

THREE TRICKS
TO WATCH FOR
(AND ONE TO IGNORE)

Single Letters

Often, a cluemaker will have a single letter to account for in a clue—a letter that can't be defined, the way a word can. For instance, suppose I want to write a clue for the word *stolid*, and I notice that the word is composed of the letter *t* inside the word *solid*. To write a container clue, I'll have to define both components: *t* and *solid*. How can I take care of the *t*?

Here's how:

Emotionless and dependable around the head of Thailand (6).

"Emotionless" is the straight definition, "dependable" is *solid*, and "the head of Thailand" is the head of the *word* Thailand—the letter *t*.

Here are some more ways I could have indicated the letter *t*:

cattail
Beethoven's fourth
the end of August
treetop
the beginning of time
Middle Dutch

The possibilities are endless, and endlessly deceptive.

Abbreviations

A simpler way for a cluemaker to account for an isolated letter or two is through the use of common abbreviations. For example:

Dance and drink, to a degree (5).

The answer is *rumba*. The wordplay—"drink, to a degree"—is a word chain: "drink" is *rum* and "a degree" is a *B.A.*

Here are the most common abbreviations you will encounter in a cryptic crossword:

Roman numerals

I, V, X, L, C, D, and M may appear in a clue as 1, 5, 10, 50, 100, 500, and 1000 respectively.

Sometimes L, C, D, or M will simply be indicated by "many" or the equivalent.

Directions

N, S, E, and W are regularly indicated by "direction" or "point" (as in a compass). Thus, "pointless impulse" is the wordplay part of a definition for *him*; it's *whim* without the *w*.

O may be indicated by "circle," "zero," "ring," "nothing," or "love" (as in tennis), among others.

Other common abbreviations:

AC and DC	(currents)
AI	(first rate: "A-one")
B/D	(born/died)
D/R	(Democrat/Republican)
E	(English)
F/P	(loud/soft: musical markings for *forte* and *piano*)
G	(thousand: gangster slang for "grand")
L/R	(left/right)
U	(proper: acceptable—as opposed to "non-U": from Nancy Mitford's essay)

Self-Reference

If you come upon a numeral in a cryptic clue, it probably means one of two things. If it's 1, 5, 10, 50, 100, 500, or 1000, it could very well indicate a Roman numeral. If it's any other number, it probably refers to the solution of the clue with that number.

For instance, suppose a puzzle has the word *caliper* at 6 across, and another clue in the puzzle reads like this:

> Duplicate 6 badly (7).

Substituting *caliper* for 6, we get "Duplicate caliper badly," an anagram clue for *replica*.

You'll see this technique used frequently in Frank L. Lewis's cryptic puzzles in *The Nation*, which, incidentally, were the first cryptics to appear in America, in 1960. (The trick is never used with a number that indicates both an across clue and a down clue.)

One to Ignore

Sometimes you'll see two consecutive clues linked by an ellipsis to form a single sentence. Here's an example:

> Inside, shear the middle. . . (5)
> . . . of the sheep and of the cows with no head (5)

This is just a little hotdogging on the part of the cluemaker. Ignore the ellipsis, and treat each clue separately. The answers to these two are *heart* (hidden in <u>shear the</u>) and *ovine* (<u>bovine</u> beheaded).

COMBINATIONS

The final fact to learn about cryptic crosswords: almost every type of clue lends itself to combination with another. One of the components in a container clue may be a reversal, for instance, or part of a word chain may be an anagram. (Double definitions and hidden words are the only two clue-types that don't work in combinations.) Here's an example of a clue that involves more than one type of wordplay:

President is not back after soccer player goes around tree (10).

This clue is a word chain with two components: a container and a reversal. "Not back" is *ton*; "soccer player goes around tree" is *wing* around *ash*, or *washing*; and the straight definition is "President." Put it all together and it spells *Washington*.

Here are some more combination clues to try. If you get stuck, turn to page 146 to find out what types of wordplay each clue combines.

COMBINATION WORKSHEET

1. Delay her about Linda's innard (6)
2. Kinds of puzzles with weird rocs and rapiers (10)
3. For comic-strip character hears sandhills resound with flawed ruby (10)
4. Greek hero's coldness in upstream waters (8)
5. Freudian therapy for severe disorder about stage of development the fourth of July (14)

To conclude this chapter, here are the six most important strategies to remember as you solve cryptic crosswords:

- Ignore punctuation in the clue.
- Look for the straight definition at either end of the clue. It will generally be the clue's first few words or last few words.
- Check closely if part of a clue seems especially outrageous or contrived; it's a good bet it's part of the wordplay.
- Be on the lookout for misleading parts of speech. A word that appears to be one part of speech in the full clue may actually be another in its true cryptic function (that is, straight definition or wordplay).

Also, don't be duped by homographs—words with the same spellings and different meanings. The word "flower" in a clue may mean *tulip* or *daisy* or *rose*, but it may just as well mean *Hudson* or *Seine* or *Thames*, all of which flow.

- Look for an anagram in any word or consecutive words with the required number of letters, especially proper nouns and contrived-sounding words.

- Never despair if a puzzle has you totally stumped. If you just set it aside and come back to it a few hours later, chances are you'll see a few answers that baffled you at first.

You now know all there is to know about solving cryptic crossword puzzles. To start you off on what I hope will be a long addiction, here are nine of the best American cryptics. All of them employ an extra gimmick, in addition to using cryptic clues. This gimmick is explained in the instructions for each puzzle. I have not selected any British cryptics since they generally contain enough cockney slang, cricket terms, and other arcane Briticisms to bog down American solvers.

Puzzle 9: Theme and Variations

(Acknowledgments to *The Listener*)

Nine lights (i.e., diagram entries) are unclued. These include three Theme Words, A, B, and C, a familiar group (one of them a two-word entry). Each Theme Word has two Variations—words related to it in some way. For instance, if the Theme Word is *Reindeer*, its Variations may be *Comet* and *Cupid*, two examples, or *rain* and *dear*, homophones of its component parts. Each Theme Word is related to its Variations in a different way.

Clue answers include one proper noun. Punctuation in the clues may be used deceptively.

ACROSS

1. Thinks, eats, wraps present (8)
6. Theme Word A
10. Period in macaronic poet's work (7)
12. Spike can puncture at the end (4)
13. Helping a couple of Mexicans with pronunciation (4)
15. Spiritual mediums with little craft losing face (7)
16. Variation on B
17. President in '50 died highly regarded (5)
19. It might be Winston Churchill's primary target—i.e., maneuvering (9)
21. Light's counterpart (5)
23. Variation on C
25. Sailor, unassisted, gets sea creature (7)
26. Crass wound marks (5)
28. Take journey around the middle of December (6)
30. Theme Word B
32. Variation on C
35. Someone with self-discipline may have skill in bridge (7)
36. Herod misrepresented in mass (5)
37. Right sort of dessert food (4)
38. The opposite of melancholy in spirit! (4)
39. A free desert (4)
40. Taking again of tinted camera shot (12)

DOWN

1. Variation on A
2. At company this would be promised discount (4)
3. Ready to run—get up and go outside (4)
4. Sign tossed out for lack of imagination (10)
5. Excitement about a way to get high (5)
6. Variation on A
7. In brook's mouth (5)
8. Born and died in poverty (4)
9. Grotesque scab covers messy, skinless wound (7)
11. Opposing view in *The Atlantic* (4)

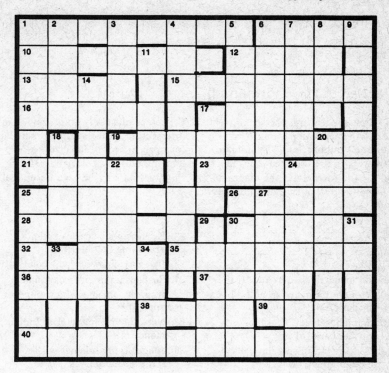

14. Theme Word C
17. Bind fifty-one (4)
18. Child born to Abraham (4)
20. Double portion of salt and one cup of a mineral substance (8)
22. Odd clue is not clear! (7)
24. About one pound, bird is light (7)
25. Someone who's like Cupid or more mischievous? (6)

27. About 101 car crashes (5)
29. Take up canvases, get fish (5)
30. Variation on B
31. Positive side to a poem (5)
33. Pointless worship? (4)
34. Appear in meeting place with speech (4)

Puzzle 10: HI (Shorthand I)

This puzzle features the sort of rebus found in the National Puzzlers' League's publication, *The Enigma*. Answers to the fourteen clues in shorthand form enter the diagram as normal words. In case of ambiguity, the solver must rely on other intersecting answers. Answers include four proper words and two uncommon words, 33A and 7D. Punctuation may be used deceptively.

ACROSS

1. TT (7)
6. Returned flushed by race (5)
10. Prepare for grave trouble—blame leader of Mob (6)
12. Some baseball players fell or turned back (6)
13. Condescend in speech to Scandinavian (4)
14. Lie back with cola on the rocks in a glass (7)
15. PA (5)
16. SR (7)
18. Part of the body wanted for headless horseman? (5)
19. $\frac{M}{E}$ (7)
21. EE (5)
22. Number of disciples practice Eastern philosophy (5)
24. *The Castle* in foreign dialect (7)
26. Checks for ladies' underwear (5)
27. Bird after night in storm (4)
30. N (5)
32. VR (4)
33. Endlessly rib seasick sailor, provoking laughter (8)
35. By exercising cure pale color (4)
37. Suspension of riper bananas in front of someone who wanted an apple (8)
38. Note about inflated East Indian money (5)
39. Judges tying tongues with sesquipedalianisms (7)
40. S (7)
41. Bucks and bolts (5)

DOWN

1. DE. (6)
2. Someone who wants a fat lip? Pop one after school (6)
3. BA (7)
4. M { (7)
5. Instrument for alerting in distress (8)
6. E (6)
7. Little island is covered with peyote (4)
8. Breed for speed (4)

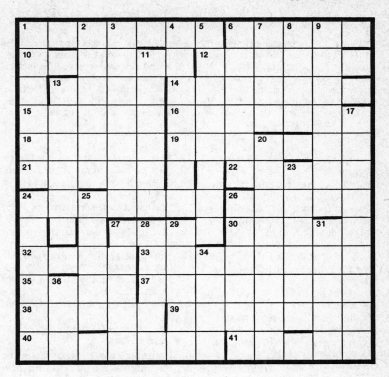

9. Bunk bed's top piece nearly toppling (7)

11. Set at an angle, burrow comes up under field (6)

13. Scopes's lawyer loses fight but gains victory for me! (6)

17. N (9)

20. In condition of poor visibility, circle hill with autopilot? (8)

23. Man-sized, shelled, cracked nuts (6)

24. $\frac{C}{S}$ (6)

25. Cross between "tweet" and "chirp" comes from dodo (5)

26. Z's point penetrates tender areas (6)

27. Over fifty, develop urge for mushy stuff (5)

28. The Earth comes up for judgment (5)

29. Subject, e.g., in story (5)

31. In 400, hail fell (5)

34. Source of starch in Christmas pudding (4)

36. Most of nice slice (3)

Puzzle 11: Noel

The answers to this puzzle's clues are to be entered letter by letter in the designated squares to form a thematically appropriate quotation, reading left to right. Spacing and punctuation in the quote are left for the solver to determine. As in the Double-Crostic format, numbers in the grid refer back to the corresponding clues and the consecutive first letters of the clue answers supply an additional message. Answers include one proper noun. Punctuation in the clues may be used deceptively.

1. Tranquil Nativity scene (6) (N3, J2, D3, K9, H10, M11)

2. Cheops prepared for ages (6) (K1, B13, H3, D4, M10, G2)

3. Hearing, for example, a declaration (6) (B1, A12, G5, N12, I8, L10)

4. Angels playing Emi harps (8) (J7, H9, K4, E13, D1, B11, M7, D9)

5. ⅙ of a sheep? (5) (A11, I14, H6, N5, H12)

6. Sign for peace in Christmas book (5) (H7, I11, K2, D5, J10)

7. Wreck moves awkwardly (8) (C15, H5, F8, K12, I4, D13, L7, B4)

8. See sign fabulously betokening birth (7) (A9, B12, L5, J9, A14, F6, C8)

9. Beating unconscious in arena (7) (N14, E7, F11, C9, J14, A2, H8)

10. Give death yelp (5) (B7, L8, M14, C2, A15)

11. Calm night (4) (K3, D14, K8, G3)

12. Gentle shepherd, e.g. (6) (M6, A13, A8, G1, D15, G10)

13. At home, make Christian observance lazy (8) (J6, C3, K5, M4, F5, C13, I6, H4)

14. Bill taking out Viking's center (4) (K7, L1, L12, N8)

15. Traveled about for $1000 extra (6) (I7, A7, L6, H15, G7, F13)

16. Wrapping present, whistle—producing "White Christmas"? (7) (F4, M8, D8, B5, E2, F12, L9)

17. Peg has unusual worth (5) (E5, G12, B8, F10, D11)

18. Hoop spun around woman's middle with enthusiasm (5) (G4, K6, J13, B3, A4)

19. Steamy ground around most of the rock (8) (L4, A6, D12, G11, C10, N2, H1, B15)

20. Section of tree ring design (4) (I9, C5, M2, N7)

21. Place and time for a type of plague (6) (J4, H14, E12, K10, L3, B10)

22. Struggle with fish (8) (D6, E4, I1, F3, N6, K14, B9, G14)

23. Harsh, interminable dry spell (5) (E14, I13, N4, L2, C1)

24. Insult from football player (6) (N11, G8, J15, I5, H2, N15)

25. Sailor with sailing team (4) (C6, N1, I10, D2)

26. The subject of egomaniacs? (5) (E1, B6, G13, I12, C11)

27. Gangster's cover (4) (L13, F2, J12, M15)

28. Patriarch's tree (5) (A5, E3, J11, L15, F9)

29. A lake in a high place (5) (K13, F7, D7, L11, G15)

30. Plant wisteria around bend (5) (M9, E6, C14, H11, D10)

31. Confine burning outside a half-mile (5) (J5, I2, L14, E15, A3)

32. Played slowly as well as before (7) (J3, M1, K15, N13, I3, H13, E10)

33. Standard seen before an English invader (6) (E11, G9, C4, M12, J1, F15)

34. Athlete's cup (7) (K11, M5, B2, F1, N9, E8, C12)

35. Brush, perhaps, around gold tooth (5) (M13, E9, M3, A10, B14)

36. Turn over information for ordering part of baseball uniform (7) (N10, F14, C7, J8, A1, G6, I15)

	1	2	3	4	5	6	7	8	9	10	11	12	13	14	15
A	36	9	31	18	28	19	15	12	8	35	5	3	12	8	10
B	3	34	18	7	16	26	10	17	22	21	4	8	2	35	19
C	23	10	13	33	20	25	36	8	9	19	26	34	13	30	7
D	4	25	1	2	6	22	29	16	4	30	17	19	7	11	12
E	26	16	28	22	17	30	9	34	35	32	33	21	4	23	31
F	34	27	22	16	13	8	29	7	28	17	9	16	15	36	33
G	12	2	11	18	3	36	15	24	33	12	19	17	26	22	29
H	19	24	2	13	7	5	6	9	4	1	30	5	32	21	15
I	22	31	32	7	24	13	15	3	20	25	6	26	23	5	36
J	33	1	32	21	31	13	4	36	8	6	28	27	18	9	24
K	2	6	11	4	13	18	14	11	1	21	34	7	29	22	32
L	14	23	21	19	8	15	7	10	16	3	29	14	27	31	28
M	32	20	35	13	34	12	4	16	30	2	1	33	35	10	27
N	25	19	1	23	5	22	20	14	34	36	24	3	32	9	24

Puzzle 12: New Directions

Instructions: The letters N, S, E and W and the pairs NE, SE, SW and NW are to be represented in the diagram by arrows suitably oriented, North lying at the top of the puzzle for Across answers and at the right for Down answers. Thus:

represents WISE and NET Across and SAW and NEAT Down.

There are no clues to the five words around the perimeter of the diagram, but these have something in common that is appropriate to the puzzle.

Answers include five proper names and one abbreviation. Ignore punctuation.

Clues

ACROSS

9. Give arsenic to each sailor's place
10. Non-pro briefly preens in the mirror, causing contemptuous look
12. Part of fur show?
13. Raised part of big reward
14. A bird that swims in a dam
15. Fellow who hangs around the French hack
16. Magazine (back issue)
17. Tossed round thing to talk about — almost
19. Charge, knowing accountant's jargon to his client
22. Take off with shrew
23. A river line which indicates direction
26. Eccentric that holds back about tie
28. Scathingly criticize cook
30. Awkward direction replaced by love for cowboy.
32. Only four, yet just beginning to be a climber
33. Crib starts to decay
34. More than one also is heard
36. Superior to South America?
37. Arrive with identification papers all dry

DOWN

1. The Queen takes it up inside in a restful state
2. Is *terra firma* a Latin conjunction?
3. The sound of the Instructions diminishes
4. Where to find the non-U patients approaching the Center?
5. Sean is confused about his country, like one who takes a gander
6. Whack after starting to whack out-of-whack
7. Put one in — nothing is secure . . .
8. . . . conversely, put nothing in—nothing is one that's celebrated
11. Run about in small English runabout?
18. Burn with sulfuric acid, hydrogen, and so on to start with
20. "Inside" picture with unknown line coming from star
21. Still crackling in the air?
24. Strayed over, strayed down
25. Worthless moles surfacing?
26. Silver and gold went to one place: this one
27. Put a hundred to one up just to make trouble *(2 wds.)*
29. Eaten up at the sight of a girl
31. Purdue gives a language course
35. Spanish agreement about the King's glider

Puzzle 13: Winners First

Instructions: There are no clues to the thirteen Across matches, but if you'd placed your bet on the first-named, you would have won in every case except for the fifth (which was a standoff) and the last (which would have depended on the match you attended).

Down Clues are normal, but solvers are warned that anything from one up to three letters may be stuffed into one square. Numbers in parentheses indicate the lengths of the answers; **(R.)** means that the answer is to be entered in the diagram in reverse, letter by letter. Ignore punctuation, which may be misleading.

Clues

DOWN

1. He who takes an odd ramble up to a small river? (12)
2. Marker of music-paper? (6)
3R. What comes back up inside the shade (3)
4. Foolish—like window-ledges? (5)
5. Speeds around right, uses horn aggressively (5)
6. Upcoming company has to get eight to start with (4)
7R. The Scots child I left out in the storehouse (4)
8. Darn sock, but not so ends of hole show first (4)
9R. Top Long Island Democrat (3)
10R. Look and laugh after a hail and farewell (5)
11. Young lady's address is put in writing (4)
12. Thanks a million for the hat (3)
13. Profit from the Seine? (3)
14. Planted a shrub fence and sat on it? (6)
15. Stealthy Oriental group grabs "ice" when there's more than one (4)
16. Dance invocation to the Sun-god (4)
17. Cause a snore by tossing and turning (6)
18. 51st catalogue? (4)
19. Porter who wrote for cabbage (4)
20. Man found briefly by Mary at the Inn? (4)
21. Wretched migraine, curtailed by half—still wretched (4)
22. May, for example, see little more than the second utmost (5)
23. Tours all over with what looks like a doughnut (5)
24. This Saint repeating this would make Einstein a German (3)
25. Something you climb up? Nonsense! (3)
26. Cry heard from an obstinate animal (4)
27. Everything allowed was obliged to go (3)
28. Crosses 16½ feet at least twice around the Circle (5)
29. Look for fallen arches? (6)
30. Without love, two girls in the middle twiddle (5)
31. Move around more in a city (4)
32. He was at the opera blasting away with the finale (4)
33. Puzzle-solver getting the sound of what's missing in the TV series? (3)

Puzzle 14: Vicious Circles II

Instructions: The answers to all Clues are of six letters. They are to
be entered radially—that is, from the circumference to the center of
the diagram—but, with the sole exception of **35**, *in mixed order*.

When the diagram is complete, the first (i.e., outer) circle will
contain a slightly emended form of one of the most famous exchanges
in literature, reading from **1** to **48.** Heavy lines indicate the separa-
tion of words.

The third circle will contain, clockwise, the name of the quotation's
author.

The letters in the second circle may be rearranged to spell THIRD
TRIAL PURR DIDN'T CHARM.

The letter in the center circle belongs to all answers. Answers to
the Clues include two proper names. Ignore punctuation, which is
designed to confuse.

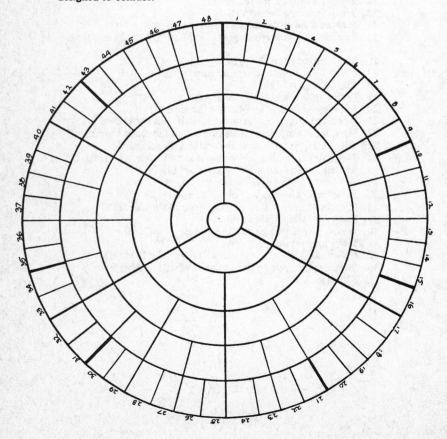

CLUES

1. Gypsy, perhaps—he can vex you
2. Former star mixing with bit players
3. Rise like a penny
4. Brown backing in the churchmen's Council
5. A lecher with polish?
6. Unusual result produced by whispering sound
7. Rested badly in bars
8. Drifts right in: takes care
9. Settle back, holding the taxes
10. A race in some eyes, they exist in all!
11. Held a session with anger and mockery
12. Mother hen, or mother's helper?
13. Sunday charges in certain counties
14. Does he fill shoes with more rubber tubes?
15. Polished lady would, shortly, being modish at heart
16. Voices disapproval of the church on the 13th or 15th of the month
17. Around 100 beheaded kings receive wounds
18. This clue is tricky: aqueduct!
19. Secure (not very!) deliverance
20. The damned dog used to be non-U
21. Part of a racer is evidently red
22. Kitchen tool for a golf dub
23. Fold around like an Indian
24. Hilarious joke delivered repeatedly by Fay Wray in "King Kong"?
25. Stopped with no difficulty in alternating current?
26. Dances, dances—get up!
27. Sketches harness connections
28. Salad holder? Sounds like it!
29. Tired lines which can be interpreted literally in Eliot
30. Stable, set in order (almost) before moving day
31. Crazy S returning in grouped force
32. Ballet composer develops block with sea-change
33. Sally has a type that is abbreviated
34. Walked along the street, then took a streetcar
35. Musical composition in the Twenties?
36. What you have to do around a trotting-horse
37. This is the club for dissent!
38. To make a mistake in missing a drink
39. For the record, the second President is a designer
40. Oyster stew from the Ground Floor, perhaps?
41. What climbing fish did and are
42. Satisfied with the small size, taking the French shoe
43. The defense is held off
44. I'm dirty: as a result, I came first
45. Diesel, perhaps, makes the bridge quickly
46. Death is half-and-half seen
47. Lo! The foot combination came through slowly
48. Races a boat around the ocean? Quite the reverse!

Puzzle 15: Chessman

Instructions: The diagram represents an elongated chessboard. Solvers are to imagine that the top row is occupied by the back row of a set of white chessmen arrayed as at the start of a game. Each of these pieces moves in the orthodox way, each move being a word, the last letter of one word being the first of the next, until it reaches a corresponding position in the bottom row. These positions will then be those of a back row of black chessmen.

Moves are clued in correct order under their respective pieces, but the length of each answer must be determined by the solver. Knights' moves, however, are all of four letters (two spaces in one direction, horizontal or vertical, and one in the other, or vice versa).

The King's journey, which follows the numbered squares in sequence, spells out the names of two famous chessmen.

The top and bottom rows contain two eight-letter words, clued first.

Answers include eight proper names and one word not found in Webster's Collegiate.

Ignore punctuation, which is designed to confuse.

CLUES

Top row: Chains of stones, linked together imaginatively.
Bottom row: One who thinks twice and goes to a pawnbroker?

KR: Life as interpreted by a friend of Lawrence's
It finally minimizes a hit that doesn't count
A crazy man held up a fish
Formerly, an attempt
Actor, poet, general, or grasping mother

KKt: Screamed out loud and stretched in the past
What failures wear
Auction off seal
What bridges cancels everything different
Symbol of effort, too backward for a lady
A friend of Abner's that might make you pucker
Calliope? Perhaps. Alley cat's cries? Sounds like both of them!

KB: Leaders of society kiss in a glider
Tossed aside mental formulations
An afterthought reflected in the Spring
Notice the first person to be the first person

Q: Mandolin brace is reversible
It's expensive, precious!
Changed and seduced again
Sidewinding tools?
Haggard old lady gives a shilling to a gentleman

QB: Just between you and me, it's nothing original
Does he stir up a traditional fall guy in suburbia?
Revolutionary high priest appears, not without being trusted

QKt: Topless, bottomless and almost due North first
Form an ideal garden out of need
A critical moment for the Devil
Abovementioned king born in a low joint
Gaelic in reverse
Look troubled about a facility
Being messed in the middle
QR: Russian actresses get British guns
Say, look! It's a Hindu
As rewritten as the dispatch
Dash off lean letters
Deserve the last first, getting close

Puzzle 16: Tossed Salad

Nine of the lights (i.e., words to be entered in the diagram) relate to other lights when they are given a 1 Across. All are common words.

Clue answers include one proper name, one proper foreign word well known from world politics, and one colloquialism. As always, mental repunctuation of a clue is the key to its solution.

ACROSS

11. Reprimand through doing an about-face on the house-top (7)
12. The full width of no longer sound trousers? (7)
13. Part of the picture, the big picture (4)
15. See 47A (6)
17. Dismounted shortly until going back (3)
19. Deer acts (4)
20. Offensive event in Vietnam? Looking back on it! It still is! (3)
21. Whip up a tale from the highland? (7)
23. This is hot in one sense—and cold in another! (5)
24. They tremble like writers (6)
25. Half of the entries in essays (5)
27. See 16D (3)
28. Talk about the derby (4)
30. An opening bid? (4)
32. Trashy singer—sounds like penny ante stuff! (5)
33. Chant when there's a change of course (5)
35. Clothing in which you reveal almost total impudence? (4)
36. See 21D (5)
38. See 21A (5)
40. Jazzy sounds, sounded like a trumpet (4)
41. Songs composed of affectations (4)
43. See 4D (3)
45. One who eats dressed in red (5)
47. Nothing more than relating to myself first (4)
48. Having smells to give up, do without? Just the opposite! (8)
49. Something anticipating refiguring of rate set (9)
50. Make another case for pantry, in relation to replacing pan (5)

DOWN

1. Liberal makes charge about King (4)
2. Sunday, pariah gets up and drives away (6)

58

3. Here's the final word on a stove pipe hat (7)
4. Observation of thousand people in bed (7)
5. Gangster's cover (4)
6. Recital in which you have to listen with soprano in actual surroundings (9)
7. Trim the tree (6)
8. Bargain time for sheets, so they say (4)
9. Starts fooling with it in a site (9)
10. One taken in by wellborn Christian (7)
14. See 28A (3)
16. One who gives tips before, not in time (4)
18. *The Informer* is—and the story of the boy with the apple on his head is too! (8)
21. Grief is only half the picture (4)
22. Advise against ad issued unwisely (8)
26. Reviles incompetent menial (7)
28. Cloth that goes around and around the ring, and all around the prizefighter (6)
29. Most of diplomacy is play (3)
31. Shelters topped off trees (6)
34. Center of earthquakes? (5)
35. The man in the fur necklace has tea that's black (5)
36. See 17A (3)
37. See 8D (5)
38. Talk up the common level (3)
39. See 35A (3)
42. Not quite appear to perceive (3)
44. Rainy part of window, etc. (3)
46. Profit from the Seine (3)

Puzzle 17: Father William—I

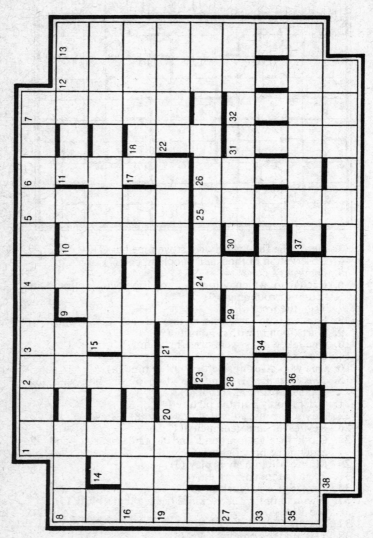

INSTRUCTIONS: The answers to clues in italics will not fit into the diagram until they become 1 Across; that is to say, each light is (so to speak) a 38 Across. (Spelling varies appropriately.) Answers include four proper names; 21 Down is a dictionary word found in Webster's.

Clues

ACROSS

1. See instructions.
8. Bears so-called approval back—too bad (6)
9. Sleeping place by an English river would reveal sleeper during tea (4)
11. Exist in primitive state—Way out! Way out! (5)
14. Foot-holds concerning a network (4)
15. *A bison used to be one, full view!* (5, 5)
16. Bent cane chairs—so sweet (10)
17. Animal and bird, from left to right (5)
19. *Fungi group, to a Doctor of Science, when put back, spoils inside* (10)
22. Cloth of Gold, but of poor quality (4)
23. *The third black minor (one being high) counting up a number of weapons* (4, 2, 5)
27. Latin actor gains a kind of support outside the palace (8)
30. Female writer's set-back, interrupting a male writer's (7)
33. Royal audience—rise up (4)
34. Siren, for example, and former ruler (5)
35. Criminal urge starts with the end of day (4)
36. It holds yards all together, I hear (4)
37. *Bowls cut profits back* (3, 4)
38. See instructions.

DOWN

1. A cargo ship fitted for resting places (10)
2. Make a hot soup—My word! (4)
3. Greeks' mount up behind, vulgarly, with nothing on (4)
4. Coming up: interminable holiday period (3)
5. Lic in hiding, skirting the Army police force (5)
6. Deals in sound cubicles (5)
7. Greek(s), however, put in time, get disgraceful mark! (5)
8. *Nation might be so addressed in speech, and go awry* (8)
9. I mouth a college movement that's short and quick (4)
10. Turn up ace and king—some split here (4)
12. *Jazzy song hit me in some degree colloquially* (9)
13. Start selecting hair accents (8)
14. *Apartment measurement when arches are gone?* (4, 4)
18. The Portuguese Left Wing (3)
20. Almost totally worn out clothes (4)
21. Exotic, bold, a coin from old Spain (5)
24. Tear the edges off land (5)
25. Wood almost links warnings (5)
26. President gives support to iron plant (4)
28. Note 1, a short procedure (4)
29. The head of a monopoly leaves deterioration (4)
31. Dance item heard in 22 (4)
32. Some mutterings in . . . Greenland? (4)

By now, W. H. Auden's favorite clue, which probably seemed mystifying at the beginning this chapter, should be more intelligible: "Song goes dry for a ruined Dean. Answer: *serenade*." It's a word chain clue in which one component is an anagram. "Song" is the straight definition, "dry" is *sere*, and "ruined Dean" is *nade*.

Not everyone who read Auden's piece in the *Times* made as much sense out of the ruined Dean. Two weeks after the article appeared, the *Times* printed this letter, from a woman named Adele Greeff:

> It seems to me that W. H. Auden, in his March 18 Op-Ed article pinpointed the difference between British and American wit.
>
> To Mr. Auden, "Serenade" has the immediate connotation of "Song goes dry for a ruined Dean," a definition compared to which those of *The New York Times* are by and large clear as flawless crystal despite Mr. Auden's complaint that they often lack precision.
>
> I am an admirer of wit, including Mr. Auden's. But the appreciation of wit depends on broad common associations. As an American, I get hung up on "ruined Dean" in Mr. Auden's example. I agree with Christopher Morley, who held it unfortunate that Plymouth Rock hadn't landed on the Puritans, yet my Puritan heritage associates a "dean" with church or college, somewhat at a remove from the open-air singing of romantic songs to ladies on balconies. Perhaps Mr. Auden knows more about deans than I do. Or perhaps "dean" has a British meaning akin to "guy"—but then I thought that this is "bloke."
>
> "Ruined" dean makes the clue even more impenetrable. Ruined how? Financially? "Bare ruin'd choirs" as an association doesn't get me anywhere either, or does it?
>
> "Song goes dry" comes through OK as "song worn out" or "useless." In American translation, is the clue trying to say that a serenade is "a useless song for an impotent guy"? If so, why don't they say so?

HINTS

Cryptic Puzzle 2

Across

1 double definition
6 double definition
9 double definition
11 double defintion
14 double definition

Down

2 double definition
3 double definition
4 hidden word
5 hidden word
7 hidden word
8 hidden word
9 double definition
10 hidden word
12 double definition
13 double definition

Cryptic Puzzle 3

Across

1 homophone
5 hidden word
7 homophone
9 homophone
12 homophone

Down

1 double definition
2 hidden word
3 hidden word
4 double definition
5 double definition
6 homophone
7 hidden word
8 homophone
10 double definition
11 hidden word

Cryptic Puzzle 4

Across

1 homophone
4 reversal
5 double definition
6 hidden word
8 homophone
9 reversal
10 reversal
11 hidden word
12 reversal

Down

1 homophone
2 homophone
3 reversal
7 double definition
8 reversal
10 hidden word

Cryptic Puzzle 5

Across

1 wordchain
5 wordchain
6 double definition
11 wordchain
12 wordchain

Down

1 double definition
2 hidden word
3 double definition
4 homophone
7 homophone
8 hidden word
9 reversal
10 reversal

Cryptic Puzzle 6

Across

2 hidden word
4 double definition
6 container
8 wordchain
10 hidden word
11 reversal

Down

1 double definition
2 wordchain
3 container
5 container
7 container
9 homophone

Cryptic Puzzle 7

Across

1 word chain
5 fragment
6 container
11 hidden word
12 container

Down

1 double definition
2 double definition
3 homophone
4 hidden word
7 fragment
8 reversal
9 fragment
10 fragment

Cryptic Puzzle 8

Across

1 wordchain
6 double definition
7 anagram
8 hidden word
11 hidden word
12 anagram

Down

1 anagram
2 reversal
3 container
4 fragment
5 homophone
9 anagram
10 fragment

2
diagramless
puzzles

Once upon a time, in the 1920s—no one is quite sure of the date—Margaret Petherbridge, Prosper Buranelli, and F. Gregory Hartswick, the three editors of the *New York World* crossword and the young Simon and Schuster series of crossword books, sat down at a Bowery restaurant called Moneta's for lunch and a session of proofreading. As the three pulled out their sheaf of papers to look over, they found that the diagram for one of the puzzles was missing—they had only brought along the accompanying list of definitions. Undaunted, and unaware of the historical significance of his action, Hartswick flipped over his menu and, with one eye on the page of definitions, proceeded to pencil in the entire diagram, fully solved.

Hartswick's serendipitous discovery is now a regular feature of several puzzle magazines and the *New York Times* Sunday puzzle page, which prints a pair every four weeks. Without question, diagramless puzzles are the classiest, most challenging, most satisfying conventional puzzle around. (I say "conventional" to leave a little room for the extraordinary cryptic puzzle.) Certainly, they have their diagrammed ancestor beat hands down. Furthermore, despite the fact that only a few publications actually print diagramless, a simple operation can transform any crossword puzzle into a diagramless: just rip the diagram out. For the weary day-in-day-out puzzle solver, this is a terrific way to break up the old routine.

Best of all, there is an absolute technique—a few rules and a few strategies—to solving diagramlesses, a technique that I will explain by working through a sample diagramless puzzle. Read the explanation once and you'll never look at a diagram again.

To begin with, here are three facts you should know about all standard crossword puzzles:

- All words are at least three letters long.
- Every letter is part of two words; that is, there are no so-called "unkeyed" or stranded letters. Each letter is part of a word going across and a word going down.
- All diagrams are symmetrical in the following way: if you rotate the diagram 180 degrees, it will look the same. In other words, every square has a corresponding square reflected across both the diagram's diagonal axes. A square two from the left in the second row from the top, for instance, will have a corresponding square two from the right in the second row from the bottom.

These rules—formally set down by Margaret Farrar (née Petherbridge)—hold for just about all published crossword puzzles. The diagramless puzzles are no exception, and as you will see, these rules are extremely important to remember.

The diagramless puzzles published in the *Times* are notable for their unusual shapes. While virtually all of them obey the symmetry rule, they are likely to have various appendages of odd shapes and sizes sticking out all over. (Of course, each appendage has its corresponding appendage on the other side of the puzzle.)

The few diagrams of diagramless puzzles that do not obey the symmetry rule are of two variations: either they are symmetrical along a vertical axis, or—and this is one of the great satisfactions of solving diagramlesses—they form a shape appropriate to the theme of the puzzle. A diagramless puzzle filled with names of notable women, for example, may be in the shape of the biological symbol for female; a puzzle appearing on Easter Sunday may be in the shape of a bunny rabbit. It is a great moment when you take another look at a seemingly obscure and shapeless diagram and suddenly a significant shape pops out at you. Five examples of this sort of puzzle appear at the end of this chapter.

But for the time being, we will concern ourselves with puzzles that do conform to the rule of diagonal symmetry. And a good starting point is a diagram of familiar proportions—15-by-15, the size of a daily newspaper puzzle. Once you see how a conventionally shaped puzzle can be solved without its diagram, it will be a short leap to go on to solve the misshapen puzzles that are published as diagramless.

This puzzle, which I constructed, appeared in slightly different form in the daily *New York Times* of December 6, 1976.

Puzzle 18

Across

1. Decorate anew
5. Spaniard's bed
9. Aid
13. Jewish month
14. October birthstone
15. Lad's date
16. "____ Like It Hot"
17. "Rule Brittania" composer
18. "____ Mad Mad . . ."
19. Oscar winner
22. Huzzah
23. Feel ill
24. Sandpiper
25. Maroon
28. Very old: Abbr.
30. Uno, ____, tres
33. Pasture sound
34. Indian nurse
35. Anger
36. Oscar winner
41. "The Snake ____"
42. Convey
43. Links area
44. Stout's relative
45. Compass point
46. Chemical compound
50. "Hallelujah ____ Bum"
52. Friend of Curly and Larry
54. Flightless bird
55. Oscar winner
61. Ginsberg opus
62. Fame local
63. Glut
64. Med. course
65. ____-de-camp
66. "A ____ Is Born"

67. Shells out
68. Nellie and others
69. Monster's lair

Down

1. Outcome
2. Certain ladder-user
3. City eyesore
4. Spread
5. Raccoon-like mammal
6. Kind of fools or showers
7. "Buddenbrook" author
8. Words with shake or break
9. "___ Doesn't Live Here. . ."
10. Part of RBI
11. He, in Naples
12. Russian leader
19. Relative of mayday
20. Aida's lover
21. Bunker and namesakes
26. Quantity: Abbr.
27. Ad ___

28. French soul
29. Snider
31. Kind of mineral
32. Sabbath talk: Abbr.
34. Tack on
36. Tax-form expert: Abbr.
37. Well or paint
38. Piano maker
38. Chemical suffix
40. Pres. Wash.
47. Conductor Zubin and family
48. Moslem nobles
49. Capek play
51. Liquifies
52. Decaying
53. Eyes
55. Bloke
56. Hebrides island
57. Pequod skipper
58. Shadow
59. Org.
60. Foie-gras offering

The first thing to do when you tackle a diagramless puzzle is to check the first two words across. In this case, they are numbered 1 and 5. This bit of information is all you need to start, as long as you know the way crossword puzzles are numbered, and this is the way: *There is a number in each square that starts a word.* Every square that contains the first letter of a word going across or down has a number. The numbers go in order running from left to right across the first row, then from left to right across the second row, and so on. You should also remember that before and after each word, there is at least one black square (unless, of course, the word is bounded by the puzzle's edge).

Now consider the top row of any puzzle. Every square is part of two words—that's one of the unbreakable rules of crosswords.

What this means is that every square is part of a word going down, and because we're looking at the top row, every square in the row must be the *first letter* in a word going down. In other words, every square in the top row of a crossword puzzle is numbered.

Let's take another look at our puzzle now, and figure out how the numbers are going to look in the top row. The first square will be numbered 1; it is the first letter of 1 across and 1 down. The square next to it will be the second letter of 1 across. It must also, we know, be the first letter of a word going down, and so it must have a number—the number 2. By the same logic, the third square must be numbered 3—it is the first letter of 3 down—and the fourth square must be numbered 4. A look at the definitions tells us that we haven't made any mistakes yet, for there is a 1 across, and there are down clues numbered 1, 2, 3, and 4—just as we have figured.

The next square presents a new twist. It is the fifth square in the top row, so it must be numbered 5, and it must be the first letter of 5 down. Checking the definitions, we verify that there is, in fact, a 5 down. However, the list of definitions contains a 5 across as well. This word—"Spaniard's bed"—must begin in the square numbered 5. Square number 5, in other words, is the start of a new word going across, and this new word must be separated from the previous word across (number 1) by at least one black square.

We now know a solid bit of information about the top row of this puzzle. The first four squares are numbered 1, 2, 3, and 4; they are respectively the first letters of 1 down, 2 down, 3 down, and 4 down; and they are the four letters of 1 across—"decorate anew." *One across, in other words, is four letters long.*

We also know that after these four squares, there is at least one black square, and then the square numbered 5—the first letter of 5 across and 5 down. (In this chapter's diagrams, a question mark represents a gap of indeterminate length.)

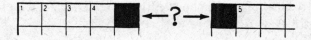

You may ask how we know there are no spaces between the first four squares. Consider what would happen if a black square did interrupt the first four squares: the letters immediately to its left would have to form a complete word. We know that a word's minimum length is three letters, so the first three letters must come uninterrupted by a black square.

How about after the first three letters? Well, suppose there were a black square after square number 3. The next square, we know, has to be number 4, and with a black square at its left, it would have to be the first letter of a word going across. But check the list of definitions: there is no 4 across.

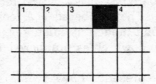

The fact is, that by the logic we have just used, we can determine a basic rule for starting out diagramless puzzles:

The number of letters in the first word going across (that is, 1 across) is always one less than the number of the second word across.

If a puzzle begins with 1 across and then 7 across, 1 across will be a six-letter word. If a puzzle starts with 1 across and 12 across, 1 across will have eleven letters. And the reason this rule holds, as we have seen, is that the squares in 1 across will always be numbered consecutively from 1 up to (but not including) the number that begins the second word across.

With this rule, we are ready to plunge into the puzzle at hand. As I work through it, my bafflement at certain words will not be altogether genuine; after all, I've solved this puzzle a number of times without much difficulty. Still, I'll try to render each step of the logic that would go into solving this puzzle for the first time. The best way to follow along is to work out each step on a sheet of graph paper, although the back of a menu seems to work just as well.

To start with, we know that 1 across is four letters long. "Decorate a new" is not an obvious clue; let's try to proceed without immediately solving it. The way to do this is to work out the down clues that cross 1 across—a task complicated by the fact that we don't know their lengths.

One down is "Outcome." This could be a few things: END and UPSHOT are possibilities; so is RESULT. Since 1 across is likely to start with RE, RESULT looks like a good bet.

Two down—"Certain ladder-user"—is a little trickier. Let's come back to it.

Three down has lots of possible answers: "City eyesore" could be TENEMENT, SLUM, POTHOLE, DUMP, or GARBAGE, to name just a few.

Four down, which will start with the last letter of 1 across, is a familiarly one to puzzle solvers; "spread" is standard crosswordese for OLEO.

We can now take a stab at 1 across. Assuming that RESULT and OLEO are correct, we have R——O and our choice is clear: REDO. Once we write this in, we can also write in DUMP at 3 down. Here's the way this corner looks so far:

	R	E	D	O		
	E		U	L		
	S		M	E		
	U		P	O		
	L					
	T					

Notice that I put a black square at the beginning and end of every word I determine.

At this point, it's a good idea to take a look at the letters below the top row for two reasons. First, make sure that they don't form any unlikely combinations in the words that are beginning to take shape. Second scan down the list of across definitions to see if any seem to fit the letters in one row.

Here, we have E-UL in the second row, S-ME in the third, and U-PO in the fourth. None of these are impossible combinations. (A combination of letters that should make you check for a mistake is something like VD-F or II-B—combinations that absolutely don't exist in any word.)

Now look at the across definitions. Nothing springs forth for E-UL or U-PO, but 16 across looks perfect for S-ME. So put a 16 in the square with the S from RESULT and pencil in the O to make SOME.

Notice that I've blackened in the square to the right of E-UL. Once I blackened in the square to the right of REDO and the square to the right of SOME, the square between them could not be part of a down word; it too must be black. By the same logic, I've blackened in the square to the left of E——UL.

A quick check you should now make is to see if there's a 16 down. The diagram we've sketched in does not leave room for such a clue; the square numbered 16 would have to be the word's first letter, and in our diagram, square 16 is in the middle of 1 down. Our check is successful; there is not, in fact, a 16 down. But every time you number a new square, check the list of definitions to make sure you haven't made an error.

Five across presents us with a major question: where is it

located in relation to the chunk of letters we've been working on? There are generally four possible answers:

- It could be connected to the chunk we have so far, in which case there are two possible locations:

1. Directly underneath 1 across, in the diagram's second row.

2. In the second row, starting to the left of the word beneath 1 across (impossible in this case since we have a black square to the left of E–UL).

- It could be unconnected to the chunk we have so far, in which case there are two further possible locations:

3. In the same row as 1 across, immediately to its right.

4. In the diagram's second row, to the left of 1 across.

In general, whenever you start on a new chunk of a puzzle—a section not immediately connected to the section you already have—you will face these four possibilities. Let's consider the three that apply here.

If choice 1 were correct, 5 down would begin with the E of RESULT. There would be no five down, because the E is already in the middle of 1 down. However the list of definitions tells us that there is, in fact a 5 down.

The remaining two possibilities are equally plausible at this stage. The best way to proceed is to try to figure out the down clues that intersect with 5 across—they should give us some idea of the word's shape and location. So let's consider 5, 6, 7, and 8 down—the down clues before the next word across.

Five down—"raccoon-like mammal"—is hard to guess.

Six down is "Kind of fools or showers," and that has to be APRIL.

Seven down is another one we can fill in; "*Buddenbrook* author" is definitely MANN.

And for eight down—"words with 'shake' or 'break'"—we can safely write A LEG.

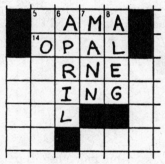

Let's see how this looks row by row. The first row, -AMA, is plausible for the Spanish word bed. Check the list of definitions to see if any across clues make sense for the second row, -PAL. Fourteen across looks very good—"October birthstone" is definitely OPAL. Let's write in the O and number that square with a 14.

With OPAL written in, we know that 5 across has to be a four-letter word; the blanks on either side of OPAL mean that any further letters in 5 across would have nowhere to go in the down direction.

At this point, faced with two possibilities for the location of 5 across and the words below it, recall that this is presumably a first effort at solving a diagramless puzzle. Recall, too, that this puzzle appeared as a conventional daily puzzle, a form in which all fifteen squares of the top row are generally filled with letters, with one or two black squares between words. Choice 4, in which the Spaniard's bed lies in the diagram's second row, would leave only four filled squares in the top row, a very unlikely set-up for a daily puzzle. So let's take beginner's license to cheat slightly and determine that choice 3 has got to be correct. In solving an actual diagramless, we would have a bit more slogging out to do before we arrived at this information, but once you've worked through a sample diagramless, the slogging will be simpler than it would be now.

We're still not sure how many black squares are between 1 and 5 across, so for the time being, let's just write in 5 across at an determinate distance from REDO, and move on to number 9.

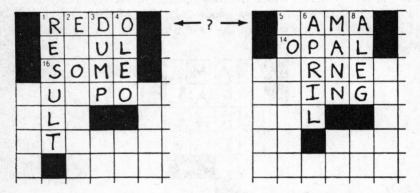

Nine across looks a bit more familiar than the clue before it, although the definition is a little too general to guess right away. Again, we face a set of four choices regarding the word's location in relation to the portion of the diagram we already have. As before, we can eliminate choice 1 (in which 9 across would be E–UL) since 9 down does exist. Faced with three other choices, we could, as we did before, assume that in a daily puzzle, this word would be on the diagram's top row, but let's proceed without making this assumption, which is how we would proceed in solving an actual diagramless.

Take a look at the intersecting down words. Nine down is definitely ALICE.

Ten down has to be either RUNS, BATTED, RUNS BATTED, or BATTED IN.

Let's skip 11 down for the time being. Twelve down has several possible answers, but let's try out the most common one—TSAR. In general, it's an excellent, almost necessary, idea to pencil in any hunch you get in solving a diagramless.

This gives us the following letters for 9 across: A--T, with the second letter an R or a B. Don't forget that if choice 2 turns out to be correct, there will be a few more letters in the middle of this word. However, even with this possibility in mind, this word is definitely starting to look like ABET. Let's pencil it in, and while we're at it, let's write in BATTED for 10 down (remembering that there may be an IN tacked on at the end). This eliminates choice 2 for this chunk's possible location. Here's how the chunk looks so far.

	9 A	10 B	11 E	12 T	
	L	A		S	
	I	T		A	
	C	T		R	
	E	E		■	
	■	D			

Take a look to make sure that the words we've written in don't give us any unlikely combinations. LA-S, IT-A, and CT-R all look plausible as components of words.

Now scan the list of across definitions to see if any match these combinations. Fifteen across—"lad's date"—looks right for LA-S; pencil in the missing S and number the L with a 15. And 18 has to refer to the movie "It's a Mad, Mad, Mad World," so write in the S in the third row and number the I with an 18.

```
 9   10  11  12
 A   B   E   T
15
 L   A   S   S
18
 I   T   S   A
 C   T       R
 E   E
     D
```

One final conclusion you should make at this stage has to do with the theme of this puzzle: even this early on, there is a suspicious number of references to movies.

Keeping in mind that we are still not sure of the location of 9 across, let's look at the next clue across. Number 13 is "Jewish month." Even with no knowledge of the Jewish calendar, we can place this clue with absolute certainty because we know there is no 13 down. This means that the first letter of 13 across—the square numbered 13—will not start a new word going down. It must be a square we already have in the diagram. Since the numbers in a crossword go in order from the left to right, row by row, the next square to be numbered is the E in RESULT, and this will become square number 13.

Now we sail for a little while. We have 14 across: OPAL. We have 15 across: LASS. We have 16 across: SOME. (Notice that there is no 14, 15, or 16 down, which checks with the diagram we have so far.).

There's no 17 down, so 17 must be the first square of -RNE. The clue is unusual—"Rule Brittania composer"—so let's come back to it. We have 18: ITSA. (Again, note that there's no 18 down.)

Here's how things look so far. (Remember that the ABET chunk could lie in the second row, to the left of 13 across.)

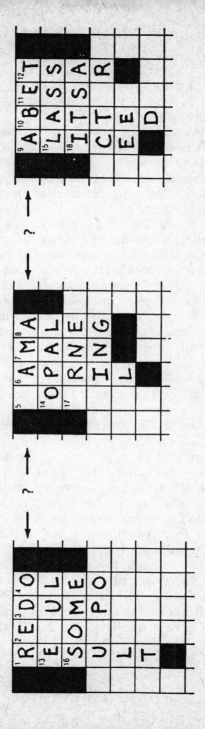

There *is* a 19 down. Now begins the trickiest and the most sensational stage of solving diagramless puzzles. Stick with this closely and the puzzle's back is broken.

Consider the possible location of square number 19. As ever, it could start an unconnected word or it could hook up to an existing part of the diagram.

But we can reject the first of these possibilities, and here is why. Suppose 19 did begin an unconnected word. It would be a three-letter word, containing squares 19, 20, and 21. Square 22 is the beginning of another word across. But figure out the diagram's width, with an unconnected three-letter 19 across. Four letters for 1 across, four for 5 across, four for 9 across, three for 19 across, and at least three black squares separating these four segments: a total of eighteen squares. We know this puzzle's width is only fifteen squares. (In all diagramless puzzles, for this very reason, you will be given the diagram's dimensions.)

So 19 across must include squares we already have in the diagram. Specifically, it must include the U-PO chunk—the next chunk over after 18 across. We also know that 19 across will include squares 19, 20, and 21—the squares that come before the next word going across. Let's examine the words going down from these squares.

Nineteen down is "Relative of mayday," and the chances are good that this will be SOS.

Twenty down is a question mark for the moment. Twenty-one down, "Bunker and namesakes," is surely ARCHIES.

Now, cast a look at the next few words across; their position may give us clues to the elusive 19 across. One fact should strike you about the next four words across: they have no corresponding word going down. Twenty-two, 23, 24, and 25 across do *not* begin with the first letter of a word going down. They must begin with a word that already exists in the diagram.

This is the fact that will clinch 19 across for us. Consider the possible fates for the -ING chunk and the CT-R chunk if they are not part of 19 across. The next word across after 19—number 22—would have to be a four-letter word with the letters -ING.

Any additional letter in 22 across would begin a word going down, and this is out of the question—the next down clue is 26. But 22 across is "Huzzah," and this looks very wrong for -ING.

But look at CT-R—it *really* looks wrong. Assuming that it is not part of 19 across, it too must be a four-letter word. (It couldn't be the tail-end of 22 across; there's no 23-down for the necessary link between the -ING and the CT-R.) And it couldn't have a fifth letter, because that would start a new word going down. Solving crossword puzzles is a game with very few absolute, exceptionless facts, but this is one: there is no meaningful four-letter combination of letters in the pattern CT-R.

The light is beginning to clear. The -ING and the CT-R must be part of 19 across. There have to be at least two squares linking these three chunks: one between U-PO and -ING, and one between -ING and CT-R. We know what these squares are, too; since 19 down (SOS) comes before any of this, 20 down must come between U-PO and -ING, and 21 down (ARCHIES) must come between -ING and CT-R.

This gives us a fifteen-letter string for 19 across, and here it is:

^{19}S U - P O ^{20}- - I N G ^{21}A C T - R

The clue is "Oscar winner," and now the answer happily pops out: SUPPORTING ACTOR.

Before we forget, we should write in any words that have poked their heads out now. Two down now looks like ELOPER, making 13 across ELUL, and 11 down has appeared in full: ESSO. Here's a diagram we have so far, stretching across the puzzle's full width:

	¹R	²E	³D	⁴O		⁵		⁶A	⁷M	⁸A		⁹A	¹⁰B	¹¹E	¹²T
	¹³E	L	U	L	.		¹⁴O	P	A	L		¹⁵L	A	S	S
	¹⁶S	O	M	E		¹⁷	R	N	E		¹⁸I	T	S	A	
¹⁹S	U	P	P	O	²⁰R	T	I	N	G	²¹A	C	T	O	R
²²O	L	E			L			R	E	E		
S	T	R					C		D	
						H		
					I	
				E	
			S	

This step is one that takes place in solving virtually any diagramless puzzle: the fusion of the chunks. It's a complicated step, but once you hash it out, it should set you up to solve the rest of the puzzle with few difficulties. Here for instances, 22 across has flowered completely; "Huzzah" turns out to be OLE.

In fact, the rest of the puzzle should take shape pretty smoothly from here on in. Using the various principles that have guided us so far, you should certainly be able to make your way to the diagram's middle. (In a 15-by-15 puzzle, the eighth line divides the puzzle in half.)

Once you reach the center line, you have two ways to proceed. You can keep hacking your way through, the way we solved the top half, figuring out the diagram from information the list of definitions gives us. Or, you can use the diagramless-solver's safety net: you can actually construct the bottom half of the diagram, since the puzzle is symmetrical.

So try working your way to the center line. On pages 91–92 you'll find diagrams that show one line more than we have so far, two lines more, three lines more, and four lines more, which takes us to the middle. (These diagrams include about half the words going down from these lines—words a solver probably would have guessed.) A solution to the whole puzzle in on page 162.

To finish this chapter, let's go over the different strategies we used in solving this puzzle—strategies that will apply in any diagramless puzzle. Here are ten basic principles to remember:

1. The number of letters in the first word across is one less than the number of the second word across.

2. Each new word is either attached to the diagram you already have, or floating on its own, to be linked up with the diagram further down.

3. Each new word is either immediately to the right of the previous word, or one row down and to the left of the previous word.

4. A clue across whose number is not also the number of a clue down must begin in a square of the diagram you already have. It cannot begin in a brand new square.

5. Similarly, a clue across whose number *is* the same as the number of a clue down *must* begin in a new square.

6. Every time you write a new word, be sure to do three things:

   a) Check the list of definitions to make sure you haven't written in a word that doesn't exist on the list.

   b) Make sure that the combinations taking shape below are all plausible.

   c) Take a look at the list of definitions to see if any across clues fit the words taking shape below.

7. Always make sure you're staying within the given dimensions of the diagram.

8. If you're stuck on a word, take a look at the next few words and come back to the one you're stuck on. Whenever you can, figure out how long a word will be—even if you can't guess the actual answer—and construct the diagram leaving unknown squares blank.

9. Once you're halfway down the diagram, you can always construct the entire diagram, following the puzzle's symmetry: the diagram will look the same if you rotate it 180 degrees. (Remember that in a few cases in which the diagram is in a special, thematic shape, this method won't work.)

10. Above all, plunge in and guess every time you have a hunch. Use

a pencil with an eraser and keep testing every possibility that occurs to you until the puzzle clicks. It's always a sensational moment when it clicks.

Here are five of the best kind of diagramless puzzles: puzzles with shapes that are appropriate to their themes.

Puzzle 19: Diagramless, 23 by 21

ACROSS

1 Frequency units: Abbr.
4 Froths
6 Molders of wasp waists
8 Red Sea crosser
10 Part of Q.E.D.
14 Of a religious season
16 Boring tool
19 Exam
23 —— seal (mystic symbol)
25 "Tell it to ——."
27 Burdensome
28 Draw —— (aim)
29 Hauls
30 One who has
31 Article
32 Comparative suffix
33 Kind of job
36 League: Abbr.
38 Cast object
39 Hebrew letter
40 Cessation
41 Formerly, once
43 Mazel —— (Hebrew wish)
44 Thy, in France
46 Indian garments
48 Kind of hose or waist
50 Slid
52 Cut short
54 Where Methuselah is mentioned
56 What one does in 66 Across
57 Asian holidays
58 Climbed
62 Kind of control
65 Prune, in Scotland
66 Jewish temple
68 Wheat particles
69 Postpone
70 One of the 12 tribes

DOWN

1 Islamic bible
2 —— the joint
3 Small food fish
4 Fairway cry
5 To-do
6 Chicago time: Abbr.
7 Sault —— Marie
8 Elected ones
9 Levy on a corp.
10 Inner: Prefix
11 —— de jambe
12 Wakeful
13 Bodies of Jewish law
14 Gehrig et al.
15 Essential being
17 Exclamation
18 Biblical mount
19 Sine —— (essential)
20 Cow's feature
21 Opera prince
22 School of Buddhism
24 Hebrew symbols
26 See 24 Down
34 —— of cloves
35 Moist
36 Copy
37 Indian weight
40 Mobs
42 Fractions
43 Make unclean
45 Discolor
46 Snow runner: Var.
47 Six, in Spain
48 Absolute
49 Sharp cry
50 N.C.O.
51 Army medal
52 Tent fixture
53 British money initials
55 Duct
56 Trouble
59 Belgian river
60 City in Okla.
61 Bewildered
62 King of Irish legend
63 Like omelets
64 Greek letters
67 —— monster

Puzzle 20: Diagramless, 19 by 19

ACROSS
1 Man on a $2 bill
10 Dos Passos trilogy
13 Candy-bar wrap
14 Correct
15 Ailment of old royalty
16 Some are gilded
17 Cockney's idol
18 Inner: Prefix
19 Early U.S. patriot
20 Observed
21 Kind of guy
22 Mideast nation: Abbr.
23 Bog
24 Obese
25 Lois or memory
26 Signifying
28 Bridge move
29 Alaskan city
30 Our uncle
31 Legislator
34 Panhandle
35 Common verb
36 Sailor
38 So. state
39 Pep
40 Kind of secret
42 Butt
43 Pronoun
44 Youngster
46 U.S. Indian
47 Disencumber
48 Consumed
49 India or printer's
50 City transit lines
51 Horn or soldier
52 Supplement, with "out"
53 Laborer
55 Tumult
56 Wily
57 American milestone
63 Bind
64 Firmness
65 Conjunction
66 All fifty

DOWN
1 Scoff
2 Sailors' saint
3 Ziegfeld
4 Dandy
5 Native of an Ionian city
6 Diamonds' country cousins
7 One who cures fish
8 Leek's cousin
9 Teachers' org.
10 Prod
11 Go to court
12 Illinois initials
13 What, in Italy
14 Narrative
16 Dative, e.g.
19 Take on
21 Flying aid
23 French painter
24 Nurtured
25 S.A. capital
26 Kind of view
27 Weight
28 Sack
30 Coal bed
31 Ditto
32 U.S. Indian
33 Seance sound
34 Like some Susans
35 British castle
37 Kinsman
38 Stove-and-kite man
39 Sheer fabric
41 Country
45 Parking woe
46 Midday pause
47 Wash. figure
54 Sparks and Rorem
55 Spanish river
58 Old-timer
59 S.A. tuber
60 Started the fire
61 Employ
62 Poetic word

Puzzle 21: Diagramless, 19 by 19

ACROSS
1 College org.
5 Light source
8 Slip away
9 Fish
10 Developed
11 Forward or lateral
15 External
17 Unpaid amounts
19 Kind of race
20 Brie, in France
21 Op or pop—
22 Connectives
23 Directed
24 Mature
26 Ordinal suffix
29 Miss Arden et al.
30 Flower child
33 Family member
36 Words describing the letter S
41 Football
scores: Abbr.
42 Of an austere season
43 Unusual person
44 Dash's partner
45 "For thee I— and balsam"
46 Network initials
49 Donkey
50 Landon
53 Like daring necklines
55 City of Italy
57 Faucet on a sink
58 Shelters
60 Duck
61 Of sight
65 Continent
66 Interrupt
67 Hurok
68 Sequoia or ash
DOWN
1 Winter ailment
2 Fabled bird
3 Mimic
4 Sorensen, to friends
5 Old French coin
6 Prefix for modern
7 More recent
8 Mr. Duchin
9 Distress call
10 Time
11 Does well
12 Equip
13 Fasten
14 Dressing flavor
16 Height: Abbr.
17 Came
18 Grange or Buttons
20 Black, for one
25 Sixth sense
26 Finial
27 Lizzie or horn
28 Men
30 S.R.O. offering
31 Chem. suffix
32 Write
33 Insane
34 Becomes talkative
35 Kind of trifle
37 Antiquity, to poets
38 Recent: Prefix
39 Explosive
40 Short flight
46 Fuss
47 Orion feature
48 Grant
50 Okla. city
51 Large moths
52 Relative of Chubby
54 School org.
55 Intend
56 Chalice veil
57 Secession initials
59 Painting
61 Month: Abbr.
62 Mongrel
63 Indian
64 — in ambush

Puzzle 22: Diagramless, 17 by 21

ACROSS

1. Culture medium
5. Stuns
10. Expansive painting
15. Hit tune by Arndt
16. Breakfast fare
18. Small African antelope
19. Yellowstone denizen
21. Dimensions
22. Man at a mike
23. Court order
25. Bump off; hit
26. Teammate of Jackie Robinson
27. Actor Erwin
28. Kind of rap or steer
29. Time, in Bonn
31. Park structure
33. Brooklets
34. Noted TV executive
35. Frosh harasser
36. Exposed
37. Listens, to Shelley
38. Kazantzakis hero
39. Fairbanks role
40. Wackier
41. Don Juan's mother
42. Caldwell or Akins
43. Army sch. for officers
46. Bolivian city
51. Branch of Buddhism
52. More serpentine
56. Surprise
57. In the bag

59. Sternmost spars on ships
61. I am present (roll-call reply)
62. Come out
63. Galley direction
64. Nominates
65. Gibber or jabber
66. Cabinet mem.

DOWN

1. Wrath
2. Songstress Eydie
3. Carroll heroine
4. Destroys
5. Money in U.S.
6. Carter and Vanderbuilt
7. Humped bovine of Asia
8. Kind of sch.
9. Interstices
10. Bryophytic plant
11. Swiss canton
12. "The Scooter" of diamond fame
13. Perpendicular to a ship's keel
14. Speech impediment
17. Jog
20. Shape of this puzzle
24. One who snuggles up
28. Shields against stains
30. Hard to handle
31. Feeds on clover
32. Was ill

34. Northern wear
35. Bar or boothbay
36. Vermont city
37. Line in the distance
38. Frigid or Torrid
39. Author Grey
40. Herzl's movement
42. Hope's "The Prisoner of —"
44. Arrived
45. Be thrifty
46. On the — (in hiding)

47. Gather
48. Cement
49. Montezuma, for one
50. Piquant
51. Biblical name for Tanis, Egypt
52. Theological insts.
53. Ending with atom
54. Poet Pound
55. Part of an army div.
58. Hoppe's stick
60. Born

Puzzle 23: Diagramless, 20 by 18

ACROSS

1. Recent
4. Headgear
7. Mr. Webster
8. Part of N.A.
9. Gaelic
10. Demure
11. Italian noble family
12. Join to
13. — fixe
14. Measure of length
15. Catch sight of
17. Lorelei's home
19. Vital fluids
20. Move suddenly
21. Land measure
22. Seethe
23. "Sweetheart of Sigma —"
24. Sight or touch
25. Former hostess

30. Swimming
32. Breathe out
34. Related through the male line
35. Objects of a hunt
39. Nickname of a southpaw
40. High
42. Old car
43. Ranges
46. Make bigger: Abbr.
47. Item of property
48. Skill
49. Chanteuse Reese
50. Stone nodules
53. Night before
54. Wriggly
55. Overflowing
56. Fifth Ave. event
60. Small mammal
62. Transmitted

63. Baseball great
64. Young boy
65. Fencing sword
66. Highway: Abbr.
67. Come out equal
68. Western state: Abbr.
69. Rocky peak
70. Indian weight
71. Military training inst.
72. Enclosure
73. Word with how or way

DOWN

1. Vikings
2. Seasonal finery
3. Cry on a roller coaster
4. Obstacle
5. Stage whisper
6. Scottish apparel
7. In want
10. Color
13. — dixit
14. Thousand, to Tacitus
15. Apiece
16. Tulips and daffodils
18. Derrick
19. Pouch
22. Throb
24. Ship's rope
25. My, to Marcel
26. Plus
27. Very thin
28. Card used in fortunetelling
29. Beverage
31. Busy worker
33. Mild oath
34. Virgil's hero
35. Raises
36. Change
37. Shrubs and grass
38. Moon goddess
39. Appendage
41. Sterile
44. Confederate
45. Utter
47. Wood used for bats
51. Italian poet
52. Chemical compound
57. Over
58. Challenge
59. British statesman
60. Greek letter
61. Word with here or there
63. Siouan

DIAGRAMLESS HINTS

one line more

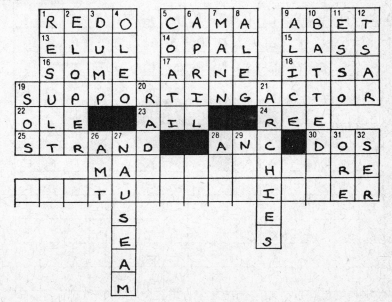

two lines more

three more lines

¹R	E	D	O		⁵C	A	M	A		⁹A	B	E	T
¹³E	L	U	L		¹⁴O	P	A	L		¹⁵L	A	S	S
¹⁶S	O	M	E		¹⁷A	R	N	E		¹⁸I	T	S	A
¹⁹S	U	P	P	O	R	T	I	N	G	²¹A	C	T	O	R
²²O	L	E		²³A	I	L		²⁴R	E	E
²⁵S	T	R	A	N	D		²⁸A	N	C		³⁰D	O	S
	³³M	A	A		³⁴A	M	A	H		³⁵I	R	E
		T	U	M		D			I	N	E	R
		S	E	D					E
		E	S						S
		A
		M

four more lines

¹R	E	D	O		⁵C	A	M	A		⁹A	B	E	T
¹³E	L	U	L		¹⁴O	P	A	L		¹⁵L	A	S	S
¹⁶S	O	M	E		¹⁷A	R	N	E		¹⁸I	T	S	A
¹⁹S	U	P	P	O	²⁰R	T	I	N	G	²¹A	C	T	O	R
²²O	L	E		²³A	I	L		²⁴R	E	E
²⁵S	T	R	A	N	D		²⁸A	N	C		³⁰D	O	S
	³³M	A	A		³⁴A	M	A	H		³⁵I	R	E
³⁶C	O	S	T	U	M	E	D	E	S	I	G	N	E	R
P	I		S	E		D		T	E	E
A	L		E	S				I	S	O
			A					E
			M					R

92

3
constructing crossword puzzles

The first thing you should know about constructing crossword puzzles is that financially it's the world's most unprofitable occupation. Always remember: If you become phenomenally gifted at constructing crosswords and reach the point where you can crank out a good one every day—a puzzle that a newspaper, magazine, or syndicate will pay you for—you could still easily double your wages by babysitting.

However—and you can be sure that the newspapers and magazines that buy crosswords know this well—the thrill of publication is the world's greatest fringe benefit. One glance at a stranger on the bus hacking away at *your* puzzle, one glimpse of a pile of publications at a newstand—and each one has *the* puzzle: these are reward enough.

But short of making it into print, there are still a lot of terrific reasons to construct crossword puzzles. There's no better gift for a puzzle fan than a stylish, professional-looking puzzle that turns out to contain his name, his dog's name, his favorite opera, or any other inside joke. Plenty of in-house publications—at schools, offices, or clubs—feature crosswords but few have really top-flight well-constructed puzzles.

Finally, there's the sheer pleasure of the construction itself. There are great moments in solving crossword puzzles—a long answer finally clicks into shape, you figure out a puzzle's theme or gimmick, you fill in the last empty square in the entire puzzle. These are the moments that somehow keep a crossword fan engaged in the same remarkably repetitive activity day after day, year after year. And yet these moments are nothing compared with the satisfactions of constructing a crossword puzzle: suddenly seeing that Alfred Hitchcock, *The Lady Vanishes*, and *Thirty-Nine Steps* are all fifteen letters long, finally coming upon a word that reads "N-blank-F," dreaming up a new way to define "emu." There are some who will scoff at this sort of discovery, but as every true crossword fan will appreciate, they are the fountain of youth, the Sutter's Mill, the double helix of the puzzler's quest.

Before we examine the technique of crossword construction, let's review the ground-rules of crossword puzzles. First, there are the regulations on the diagram, which we discussed in Chapter 2:

1. Every word is at least three letters long.
2. No letter is unkeyed; every letter is part of a word across and a word down.
3. The symmetry of the diagram is such that if you rotate it 180 degrees, it will look the same.

One additional rule to keep in mind: daily-sized puzzles are fifteen squares by fifteen squares; Sunday puzzles almost always have twenty-one or twenty-three squares to a side. At any rate, virtually all published crosswords are square, with an odd number—from fifteen to twenty-three—to a side.

You should also know, as a constructor, that many crossword editors have limits to the number of words that can appear in a puzzle. This keeps black squares to a minimum and allows for longer words. The current maximum for a daily puzzle at the *New York Times* is 76 words (78 if the puzzle has a theme), and most other publications have maximums in this neighborhood. (For a 21-by-21 puzzle, the *Times* limit is 140 words; for a 23-by-23 puzzle, it's 170.)

In addition, here are a few generally accepted guidelines concerning the words you use in a puzzle:

- Avoid commercial names: names of companies, brand names, and so on. In the puzzle about Oscar winners that I had constructed, I had originally defined ESSO as a gas company and ELAL as an airline. When Will Weng, the puzzle editor at the *Times*, was through with it, ESSO was "He, in Naples," and ELAL became the Jewish month ELUL.

- Avoid, if possible, names of diseases and other forms of suffering. The rationale for this rule is simply that a crossword's intention is always to divert and entertain, an end that is likely to be thwarted by an overdose of grim answers. This is a rule that can be prudently broken in dire circumstances—if absolutely the only word that will fit in a certain slot is *hairlip*, for instance—but it's worth making an effort to keep this sort of thing out. Try "Zodiac crab" instead of "malignant tumor"; turn your hernias into Hermias.

- Use obscure crossword-puzzle-words sparingly. Once you try constructing a puzzle, you'll see that the very words you once reviled as a solver are now treasures; there's nothing like an anoa or a ria to squeeze you through a rough crossing. But never lose your solver's perspective; it's words like these that give crossword puzzles a bad name. At the very least, be absolutely sure that two such words never cross—their square of intersection will be hopelessly out of reach.

The following excellent suggestions are from the guidelines Will Weng wrote up when he was puzzle editor at the *New York Times*.

Phrases are fine if they are reasonably familiar or logical, but avoid artificial ones such as "was in session" or "greet friends."

Go easy on proper names, especially first names that can be defined only as "girl's name," or names of people who are in the news now but who may be all but forgotten in a matter of months.

Also avoid . . . strained "re" words ("rehesitate," "redrown").

In the shorter words especially, see if the rarer letters can be used to get away from a parade of *s, r, e,* and *t* words.

Finally, suggests Mr.Weng, "look for words and phrases that you think the solver might find interesting. Words such as 'assessment' or 'reinvestigations' are not likely to provide much of a lift."

Confronted with a blank piece of graph paper, a crossword constructor has a number of possible ways to proceed, and the method you choose will depend on how you resolve a basic philosophical dilemma.

There are two schools of thought on the subject of crossword construction—two schools that diverge over a familiar dispute: form versus content. On one side are a group that might be called the structuralists, who hold that the most important feature of a crossword puzzle is its diagram. The construction of a crossword, according to this school, should ultimately be directed toward a compact and visually pleasing diagram, one with few black squares, many long words, and several sorts of symmetry. The most influential proponent of the structuralist doctrine in recent years has been Dr. Eugene T. Maleska, the *Times*'s puzzle editor. Under Dr. Maleska, the *Times*'s daily puzzle has typically been a geometric marvel, but often at the expense of an interesting theme.

On the other side is the materialist school. Materialists would gladly give up a well-crafted diagram for unusual and satisfying words in a puzzle, and above all, an appealing theme running through.

Of course, the ideal puzzle is one that satisfies both parties: a slew of long, classy words linked together in some remarkable pattern. But short of this best of all possible crosswords, puzzles tend to fall into one of the two schools. And before constructing a puzzle, it is important to declare yourself with one side or the other, for this choice dictates the first step you take in crossword construction. If you align yourself with the structuralists, you will probably want to design a terrific diagram first and then set about filling it with words. If you declare yourself a materialist, chances are you'll start out by finding a theme for the puzzle.

As I am wholeheartedly with the materialists in this debate, this second method is the one I will discuss. The puzzles I admire and remember are not four-way symmetrical, long-worded blank-less wonders; they are the puzzles that feature three or four variations on an intriguing theme—an author's works, an actor's movies, the lines of a poem, some kind of wordplay.

I'll never forget the puzzle from a daily *Times* years ago in which the long answers were defined "First part of message," "Second part of message," and so on. The complete message turned out to be something like "April Fools, there's no message in this puzzle," and of course, the puzzle's date was the first of April. Perhaps the most awe-inspiring daily puzzle I've ever come across hinged on an unbelievable theme: the three long answers, all fifteen letters, were SEVENTEEN ACROSS (the number of the clue for that answer), FIFTEEN X FIFTEEN (the puzzle's dimensions), and SEVENTY-TWO WORDS (the puzzle's word count).

So the first thing you should do to construct a crossword puzzle is choose a workable theme. For a daily-sized puzzle, a good theme should have at least three variations. The puzzle's symmetry requires long answers to come in pairs of equal lengths, but you can use an odd number of variations if one of them runs across the middle. The symmetry also dictates that a word across the middle has an odd number of letters, so that the number of blank spaces on either side of it will be the same.

As you can see, it takes a little digging and manipulating to find a theme that will satisfy these restrictions. One result of this is that a few phrases that work out particularly well have become pretty hackneyed by now. Here are some overworked fifteen-letter answers you might as well avoid:

Ernest Hemingway, *The Sun Also Rises*, and *A Farewell to Arms*.
Thomas Jefferson, Independence Day, and Statue of Liberty

"Once in a blue moon" seems to turn up almost monthly and

it's well known by now that "crossword puzzle" has fifteen letters, a fact that is nevertheless slightly eerie.

In general, most well-known personalities, places, titles, and sayings have had more than their fair share of ink. Try working in recent names and phrases, keeping in mind Mr. Weng's warning not to construct a puzzle around flashes in the pan. (Or "flashes in the pan," for that matter.) Remember that in trying to make a theme fit, you can always leave out articles (the definition will read "With 'The', . . .") or break answers up into two or three parts (like "The Adventures of" and "Huckleberry Finn").

The best way to explain the steps and strategies of constructing a crossword puzzle is to show the different stages of an actual puzzle under construction. As an example of the first effort, let's take a look at the puzzle I constructed about Oscar winners, which appears in Chapter 2. This puzzle is by no means an expert work of construction—it's cluttered with three- and four-letter words and it has a healthy dose of unwelcome abbreviations and foreign words. However, the puzzle's basic structure is the best one, I think, for a beginning puzzle: three parallel long answers.

Having chosen three long variations on a theme—categories of the Academy Awards—my first decision is how to array these three answers in the diagram. One of them must go across the middle and the other two must be equal distances from the middle. Arbitrarily, I'll decide that the three answers should run horizontally.

Now I have to decide where to place the two long answers that do not run across the middle. Consider what would happen if they ran across the very top and bottom rows. Since every letter of the long answers must be part of a word going down, and since every word has to be at least three letters long, the words going down from the long answers would form at least two more long answers. There could be no black squares in the second and third rows from the top and bottom. (The dots represent spaces that will eventually be filled by letters.)

S	U	P	P	O	R	T	I	N	G	A	C	T	O	R
•	•	•	•	•	•	•	•	•	•	•	•	•	•	•
•	•	•	•	•	•	•	•	•	•	•	•	•	•	•
C	O	S	T	U	M	E	D	E	S	I	G	N	E	R
•	•	•	•	•	•	•	•	•	•	•	•	•	•	•
•	•	•	•	•	•	•	•	•	•	•	•	•	•	•
C	I	N	E	M	A	T	O	G	R	A	P	H	E	R

The same gnarl occurs if you try to place a long answer in the second row; the crossing down-words unavoidably fill the third row with letters, there's no room for black squares in the third row, and once again, you've got one long answer on top of another.

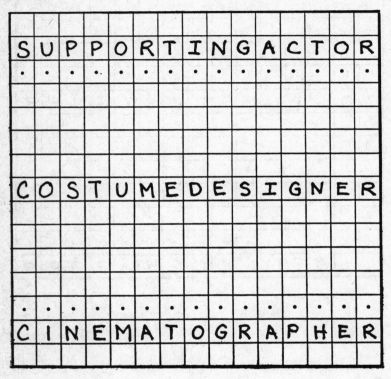

Finally, the seventh and ninth rows are out of the question for a long answer; this also produces an unwelcome mass of three contiguous long answers.

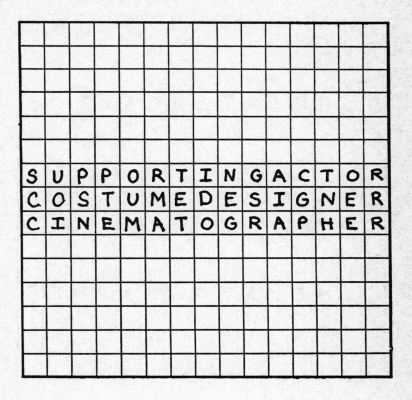

This leaves the third, fourth, fifth, and sixth rows—from the top and from the bottom—as ideal locations for a pair of long answers. For my puzzle, I picked the fourth row from the top and the bottom simply because this arrangement leaves the most breathing space possible on either side of a long answer.

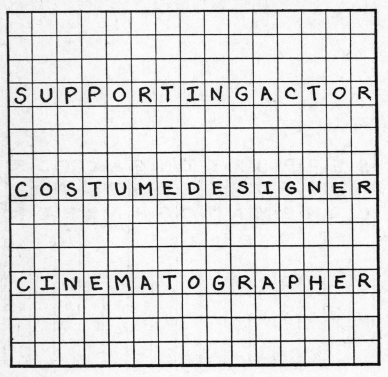

(The decision about how to order the three long answers was totally arbitrary.)

I now have the puzzle's skeleton; what remains is to put some flesh on the bones.

The best way to tackle the puzzle now is to work from the middle out. The edges of the puzzle will turn out to be easy to manipulate—add a letter here, change a letter there. But in the center of the puzzle, where so many different segments converge, any change is likely to set off a chain reaction of adjustments that will be impossible to make without changing the central long word. Better to determine the center first, and then everything else will fall into place.

Take a look at the square in the dead center of the puzzle—the D of COSTUME DESIGNER. That D is going to have to be part of a word at least three letters long. We also know that any letter above the D will have to be counterbalanced by a letter below, because of the puzzle's symmetry. So we know that at the very least, there will be a letter immediately above and below the central D. I'll put a dot above and below the D to indicate that these squares will eventually be filled.

Next, I want to make sure that all the other letters in the central answer—COSTUME DESIGNER—are part of a word going down. Some will be the first letters of a down word, some the last, and some in the middle. Assigning every letter of COS-TUME DESIGNER to one of these categories is a crucial step for two reasons. First, it assures that the middle row is safely incorporated into the puzzle, with no stranded letters that don't belonng to down-word at least three letters long. In addition, the puzzle will begin to take a more definite shape—I'll start to have a hazy idea of how the words are going to look in the center of the diagram.

So, I want to look at the rows immediately above and below the middle row and decide which squares will have letters and which will be black. Remember that every move I make will trigger off a shadow move on the other side of the puzzle. For each square I fill in the top left, I'll have to fill a corresponding square in the bottom right, and vice versa.

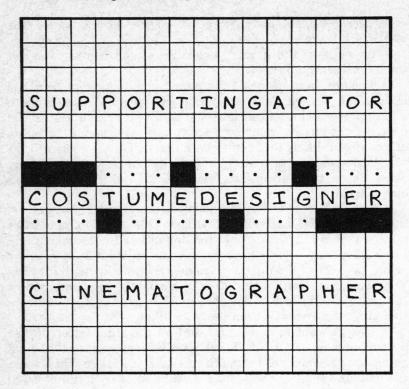

After testing out a few different arrangements, the above pattern is the one I hit upon.

One reason I chose this pattern is that it leaves room for a number of short words. Admittedly, it would be classier to choose a pattern that avoids three- and four-letter words, but for a beginning puzzle, simplicity is of the essence.

Notice that this pattern follows the rule of symmetry: it will look the same if you flip the diagram 180 degrees.

These two rows turn out to dictate a little more about the puzzle's shape. To make sure that each word is at least three letters long, we should put in the following ten dots. (From here on in, I'll circle newly added dots.)

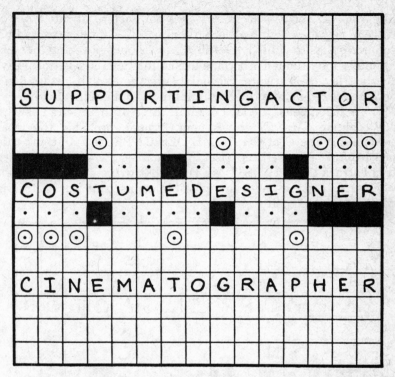

The general rule for dotting is that whenever a letter (or dot) is up against a black square (or a border) on one side, you must pencil in two dots in the other direction. Note that this rule does not hold for every empty square next to a black square—the empty square could always become black itself.

The next step is to link the three long answers. I want to find a word, or chain of words, that will connect SUPPORTING ACTOR to COSTUME DESIGNER and a corresponding word or chain that will connect COSTUME DESIGNER to CINEMATO-GRAPHER.

There are thousands of different ways to do this, but one important guideline helps focus the procedure: take care of the unusual letters. Start out by figuring out the fates of any letters like **J, Q, X,** and **Z**—letters that are not easy to fit into a word. As soon as you pencil in a word, the flexibility of the surrounding squares starts to vanish; a letter that was once hovering indeterminately may suddenly become locked into a fixed position—say, the last letter of a word. So make sure that tough letters don't become locked in like this, and manipulate them in the bud.

As it happens, the letters in all three of these long answers are common ones. Of all of them, though, probably the least tractable is the U of COSTUME DESIGNER, so I'll attack this one before I do anything else. The puzzle's symmetry requires that I attack the I in COSTUME DESIGNER. too, while I'm at it.

After testing out a few possible connecting words, this is what I come up with:

Immediately, I'll pencil in the dots and black squares that these two words require: black squares above and below the words, and four dots to make sure that every letter is part of a three-letter word in both directions.

This is what the diagram looks like now.

Notice that once I drew in the black square above the A of ARCHIES, I had to blacken in the two squares above, since they would otherwise contain a two-letter word. The same conditions hold for the squares beneath the M of NAUSEAM.

The next task to attend to is the fate of the puzzle's central square. It's best to lock this pivotal square in place first and then worry about the words that emanate from it—not the other way around.

I know that the D has to be the middle letter of a word at least three letters long. Opting for the simplest possibility, a three-letter word, I'll write in ADD. The black square above it requires a dot to its right; the black square below requires a dot to its left.

Looking at the diagram, I see I'm going to need a pair of four-letter words that read A--H and S--D. Ideally, the letters of these two words and the letters of COSTUME DESIGNER that they touch will form vowel-consonant pairs going down. This is a good principle to keep in mind: words fall into place easier when vowels and consonants alternate.

The two words I choose are AMAH and SEND. Here's how the diagram looks with these two:

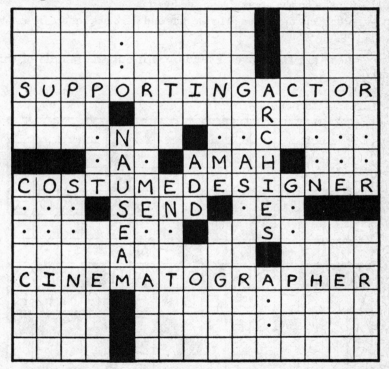

The diagram is starting to look solid now around the middle, and it is at about this point that you get the first flash of a picture that will sustain you through the rest of the construction: you can actually imagine someone sitting down and solving this puzzle. "Something-or-other down: '*Ad*-blank,' must be 'nauseam.' . . . how about the four-letter word with the S . . . 'Convey,' let's see. . . ."

Now to fill out the middle of the puzzle, between SUPPORT-ING ACTOR and CINEMATOGRAPHER. There are four things to keep in mind as you hack your way through a puzzle's belly:

- Be sure not to make a move that leaves a letter stranded—contained in only one word.
- Be sure not to make a move that leaves a two-letter word.
- Remember that for every move you make, there is a shadow move to make on the other side of the puzzle.
- After every move, pencil in the dots and the black squares the move triggers off.

These are the moves I made to fill out the middle of this puzzle:

1. *RADAMES and NASTIER*

This is a potent move. Watch what happens now.

The black square above the R of RADAMES triggers off black squares in the two spaces above it. The same conditions hold for the squares beneath the R of NASTIER. (This is the same thing that happened above ARCHIES and below NAUSEAM.)

These black squares in turn trigger off another set of eight dots, for once they are in the puzzle, the dots above the O of SUPPORTING must form words to the left, and the dots below the A of CINEMATOGRAPHER must form words to the right.

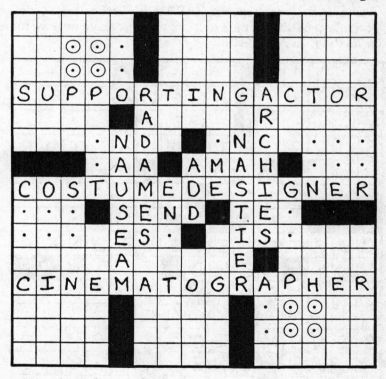

Furthermore, the black square above NASTIER sets off two chain reactions:

First, it requires two dots to the right of the R in ARCHIES. (And the blank below RADAMES requires two dots to the left of the A in NAUSEAM.)

Second, it requires two dots above the G in SUPPORTING. These dots, in turn, must form words to the left, so each of them needs a pair of dots at its side. As ever, the shadow move must be made below.

The final consequence of RADAMES, is that the A, walled off on its left, needs two dots to its right. (The shadow move takes place at the E in NASTIER.)

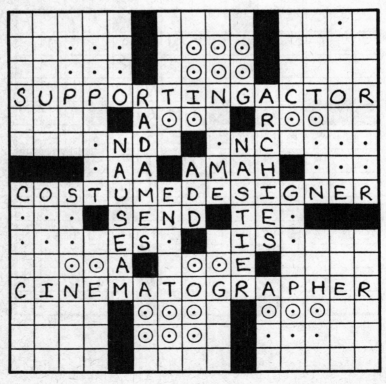

So far, I haven't run into any trouble. Trouble would come up if, say, in the various trigger and shadow moves, I were left with a dangling letter or a two-letter word, in which case I would have to scrap the problematic move. But for now, I can proceed.

2. *AMT and MAA and the shadow-move TEE and GEO*

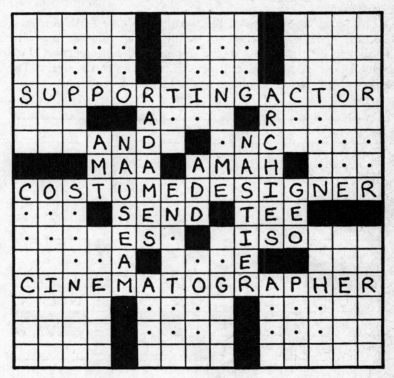

The AA that NAUSEAM and RADAMES produced was unusual enough that I wanted to get it out of the way. (Note: for the time being, I'm leaving AND and ISO alone, in case I want to incorporate them in longer words.)

3. *ANC and AME and the shadow-move ESE and ENE*

This move requires a black square above AME and one to the right of ANC (plus the two shadow black squares). In addition, it triggers off three dots in the upper right-hand corner; the dot above the C in ACTOR triggers off two dots to its right. (Three dots are also required in the lower left-hand corner.)

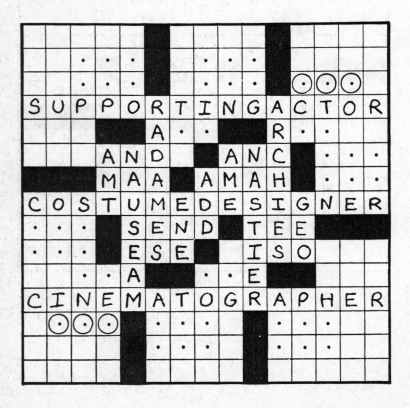

And that's the ballgame. The diagram as I have it now is the final diagram, except for six black squares I added to each half of the puzzle to make a few words shorter. Here's the diagram with the additional black squares, and dots in the remaining empty squares:

The empty squares that remain in the diagram are in six separate chunks. As a result, we can pull them out and attack them individually, piece by piece, and this is what the game of word squares is all about.

Word Squares

Word squares are the proof—as if any were needed—that crosswords are no transitory fad, but a recreation that has endured for thousands of years, and will surely outlast such diversions as skateboards, football, food, and shelter.

In its broadest meaning, a word square is any small block of letters that is roughly rectangular—a self-contained chunk of a crossword puzzle, in other words. The standard definition of a word square, though, is its purest form: a block of letters that is actually square. A good deal of history, legend, and mystery has come to be associated with this sort of word square, and it is, without a doubt, a direct ancestor of modern crossword. Before we polish off the puzzle under construction, it is worth digressing for a moment on the subject of the pure word square.

There are two breeds of these squares: in some, the words going across are the same as the words going down; in others, every word is different. The simplest possible word square is a single letter, which invariably reads the same horizontally and vertically (and out into the third dimension, for that matter). There is probably an argument to be made that the *simplest* possible word square is a blank page; such a proposition is probably best left to theologians, and not to word-players.

At any rate, word squares come in sizes up to size 9-by-9. Starting at about size 7, though, the squares begin to lose their charm and accessibility. Still, a large word square—particularly one that uses the same words across and down—is a feat of extraordinary difficulty, and for the record, here is one of the best of the giants. This square was constructed by Wayne Goodwin, a Chicago wordplayer who died in 1940. It is one of countless astonishing word squares to be found in Dmitri A. Borgmann's *Language on Vacation*.

```
F R A T E R I E S
R E G I M E N A L
A G I T A T I V E
T I T A N I T E S
E M A N A T I S T
R E T I T R A T E
I N I T I A T O R
E A V E S T O N E
S L E S T E R E D
```

The genius—and maniac—has not yet appeared who can construct a size 10 word square. However, a size 3 or 4 word square
is not difficult to construct, a fact you can easily verify. It's hard
to say which sort of word square is easier to put together—one
with the same words across and down or one with all different
words—but find out for yourself: try constructing a few of each.

The word square's historical interest has to do chiefly with
one remarkable example, whose even more remarkable history
is chronicled in Roger Millington's *Crossword Puzzles: Their history and their cult.* This is how it looks:

```
S A T O R
A R E P O
T E N E T
O P E R A
R O T A S
```

The square's first distinction is that it forms a complete
sentence, in Latin. The English translation is roughly "*Arepo* the
sower holds the wheels with force." (*Arepo* is a Celtic word for
plow.)

Its second distinction is more amazing: it is possible to read
the sentence four different ways in the square. But beyond the
square's intrinsic interest, it has the following incredible history:

In 1933, archaeologists discovered several examples of the
square in the ancient Mesopotamian city of Dura-Europos.

Three years later, archaeologists evacuating Pompeii found it inscribed in plaster on a preserved pillar.

A British vicar has reported that in the church of St. Gidding, of the diocese of Ely, an octagonal piece of oak, with the date 1614 carved at the top, bears the square.

A certain Sir Ernest Wallis Budge, writing to the *London Times* in 1929, maintained that the Sator square exists in sixth-century magical texts of the Coptics, and added that in "Lefa fa Sedek," the Ethiopian Book of the Dead, the square is said to stand for the five nails of the cross. Finally, Sir Ernest wrote, in Glamorgan, Wales, reciting the square is believed to cure the bite of a rabid dog.

What is the source of this square's mythic resonance, its pan-cultural allure? Scholars have contrived all sorts of anagrammatic significance to the square's five words. One German writer of the 1920s decided that the letters were an arcane rearrangement of this cross:

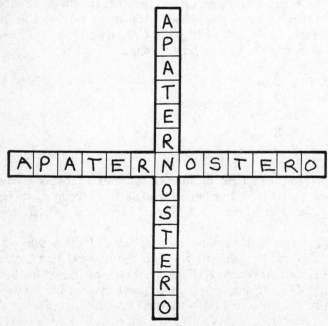

The A and the O, he argued, represent alpha and omega.

I think it is clear that the Sator square is just one especially convincing demonstration of the powerful appeal of crosswords. Twentieth-century man carves millions of word squares daily, and for more cryptic reasons than their literary significance or their religious value. Puzzles not too remote from the Sator square have been known to cure depression, tension, and fatigue—why not rabies?

One last word about word squares before applying them to the unfinished puzzle. They appear in various books as miniature crossword puzzles, with definitions given for the words, often in a short piece of doggerel. An amusing example of such a rhyme appears in Edmund Wilson's *Night Thoughts*. (It is also an encouraging instance of a less than consummately constructed puzzle finding publication and fame.) The first five clues refer to the horizontal entries; the next five to the vertical entries.

> My *first* is a garment that fastens behind;
> My *second* applies to a lush little lake;
> My *third* in your *Handwörterbuch* you will find
> May mean whilst or because; my *fourth* is a fake:
> The Association of Impotent Old Apoplectic Parties;
> My *fifth* is the steamship *Nigerian Royal Highness*;
> My *sixth* a confection of musical art is;
> My *seventh* an organ remote from the sinus;
> My *eighth* is a painter fantastic and French;
> My *ninth* is exclaimed at a wrench or a stench;
> And my *tenth* is a nimble but mythical wrench.

The word squares we will encounter in constructing crosswords are not perfect squares. Nevertheless, the process of filling in the islands of empty squares that remain in this chapter's puzzle is no different from the process of constructing pure word squares.

The only notable difficulty in constructing complex word squares—in filling these islands—is that generally, a row or column is unalterably fixed, a segment of a longer word that you won't be able to change. This handicap takes some getting used to, and later in the chapter is a series of exercises in constructing word squres with a few letters locked in.

Here are a few tips to keep in mind as you construct complex word squares—in the exercises that follow and in the crosswords you will construct.

- Try to alternate vowels and consonants.
- Test every letter that could possibly fill a given space. Jot down all the letters that fit going across and all the letters that fit going down, and compare the two lists.
- The big secret to filling in word squares, and in fact, to crossword construction in general: *use a crossword dictionary.* The best of these is the *Dell Crossword Dictionary.* In the back of the Dell is a section called the word-finder, prepared as an extra aid for cross-word solvers. The word-finder consists of virtually every legitimate three- and four-letter word, including foreign words, proper nouns, and abbreviations. The words are organized by two-letter combinations; if you have the first two letters of a word, the second and third letters, or the last two, you can find a list of all the words that use that combination.

  Certain other crossword dictionaries include this feature—some list words of five and six letters as well. However, any five- or six-letter word you have to find in a crossword dictionary probably shouldn't be in your puzzle. The Dell is compact and inexpensive and should be more than adequate for any constructor. (It also serves its intended purpose admirably, and is a great way for a beginning solver to become acquainted with the peculiar language of crosswords).

Now try working out the following exercises in word square completion:

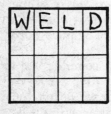 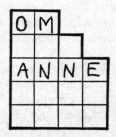 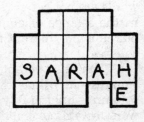

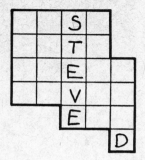

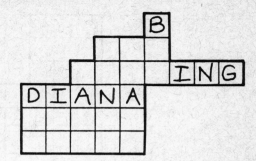

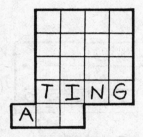

This last one is unusually tough. It should also be familiar; it's the upper middle island of the unfinished puzzle. Here are the other five word squares to be filled in before the puzzle is complete. See if you can improve upon the solutions I came up with.

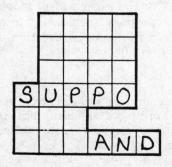

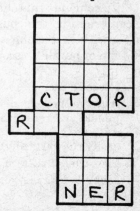

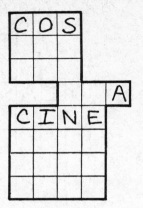

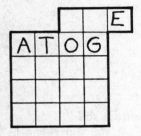

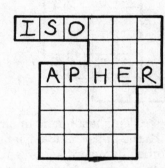

To conclude this chapter, let's review the various steps I took in constructing this puzzle. These steps refer specifically to a puzzle with three long answers that run in the same direction—the type of puzzle I recommend for a first effort:

1. Choose a theme.
2. Arrange the long answers in the diagram. One will run across the middle and the other pair will run in the third, fourth, fifth, or sixth rows from the top and bottom (the long answers can just as easily run vertically).
3. Figure out a pattern for the middle three lines.
4. Link the long answer in the middle to the other two.

5. Take care of the middle square; make sure it is part of a word at least three letters long.

6. The long step: flesh out the middle. Work from the center out and take care of unusual letters and combinations first. Remember that after every move you make, you should do two things:

- Make the shadow move on the other side of the puzzle.
- Pencil in the dots and black squares the move triggers off.

7. Fill in the word squares that remain on the upper and lower edge of the diagram.

After a puzzle or two, try expanding upon this format. Cross your long answers, run them in consecutive rows, try a Sunday-sized puzzle or a diagramless. For more than half a century, all over the world, people have been constructing crossword puzzles, but there's still ground to be broken: a crossword with no black squares, a puzzle where every word is part of the theme. . . .

4
double
crostics

When an English teacher named Elizabeth Kingsley constructed the first Double Crostic in 1934, she brought it to the New York offices of the *Saturday Review of Literature* and announced, "I've invented a new type of crossword puzzle."

Mrs. Kingsley's true vision of her invention was loftier than she let on. She had been unimpressed when the crossword became the national passion in the 1920s. "How futile," she said once, at the height of the crossword craze. "There is a certain fun in the thrill of a puzzle, to be sure, but what is the goal?"

And so she devised a puzzle with a goal—a puzzle that, as she put it, "stimulated the imagination and heightened an appreciation of fine literature by reviewing England and American poetry and prose masters." The very first Double Crostic, which the *Saturday Review* printed on March 31, 1934, was a typical Kingsley stimulant, containing this quotation:

> And tho'
> We are not now that strength which in old days
> Moved earth and heaven; that which we are, we are;
> One equal temper of heroic hearts,

> Made weak by time and fate, but strong in will
> To strive, to seek, to find, and not to yield.
> Alfred Lord Tennyson, *Ulysses*

Double Crostics have come a long way since then. This is the quotation from a puzzle in the Sunday *New York Times* of July, 1981, constructed by the incumbent guardian of the crostic, Thomas Middleton:

> Luncheon . . . was disorganized . . . Groucho expatiated . . . on his stock-market losses, Chico kept jumping up to place telephone bets, and Harpo table-hopped all over the dining room, discomposing any attractive lady who gave him a second glance.
> S. J. Perelman, "The Marx Brothers"

No doubt Mrs. Kingsley would be mortified. But it would gratify her to know that her "new type of crossword puzzle" now enjoys a secure reputation as the salutatorian of word games— "the other puzzle" for a legion of crossword fans. A regular feature of the *Saturday Review* until 1982, double crostics now appear every other week on the bottom of *The New York Times*'s Sunday puzzle page, in *Harper's* and in all puzzle magazines.

For crossword solvers whose struggle with the long, ambiguously defined, often obscure words of the double crostic remains unsuccessful, there is only one easy answer: use every reference book you can get your hands on. This method undoubtedly violates many solvers' senses of fair play, and there are those who will call it cheating. In the spirit of Mrs. Kingsley, I prefer to look at it as a kind of self-improvement.

The fact is, while there are a few good strategies to keep in mind as you solve double crostics (which I will discuss later in the chapter), there is no single underlying method to learn. Double crostics are unique among crossword-variants in this respect. In a diagramless, you have to learn how to figure out a word's length and its location in a puzzle; in a cryptic puzzle, you have to learn the different kinds of wordplay involved in the clues. A double crostic is lonelier; it's just you and the definitions. Just as in solving conventional crosswords, if you're stuck on a word, it's not because you don't know something about the way the puzzle works (as it might be if you were stalled on a word in a diagramless or a cryptic). If you're stuck, you're stuck, and you can move on to another word or reach for a dictionary.

In a crossword puzzle, there are plenty of words to move on to, and each word you figure out gives you the letters of a few more words. A double crostic has only about twenty-five words in all—twenty-five places to get started, or to move on to when you're stuck. Furthermore, in a double crostic, each letter is only part of a single solution; one answer does not necessarily trigger off another.

So take heart, and take all the help you can get. Pretty soon, you'll become familiar with the format of double crostics: the language of the definitions, the frequency of letter-combinations, the interplay between the clues and the quotation. And eventually, you'll be able to wean yourself off the reference books.

Here are a few strategies you will find helpful as you work your way through a double crostic:

- Use a pencil, and write in *any* answer that sounds right and has the right number of letters. The answer may eventually prove to be wrong, but you'd be surprised how many wrong answers have a few correct letters—letters that help the quotation take shape.
- In the same spirit, write an A in every one-letter slot in the quotation.
- Similarly, put AND and THE in the quotation as soon as one letter of either word appears.
- If a long word in the quotation has a last letter G or a next-to-last letter N, fill in two more letters to make the word end in ING. And if a long word ends with an N, or has a next-to-last letter O, or a fourth-to-last letter T, fill in three more letters to make the word end in TION.
- For the clues: write an S at the end of every word with a plural definition, and RE at the beginning of every word whose definition calls for a word meaning "do something *again*."
- Try this trick if you already have a few answers to the definitions and one particular answer is on the tip of your tongue: For each

letter in the answer, look at the corresponding letter in the quotation and see if any letters look especially likely. If there are three or four strong candidates for the slot—if it's not sitting right in the middle of a long, empty word—jot down these possibilities in a column. For instance, if the letter appears in the quotation as the first letter of a three-letter word, you might jot down a T (THE) and an A (AND or ARE).

When you have a column for every possible letter in the word (a few letters are bound to draw blanks), and all the columns are arranged in the order their letters appear in the word, read horizontally. If the trick works—and it does surprisingly often—the correct answer will pop out at you.

Constructing double crostics is another story: there's a method to it, and it's simple to learn. An unfortunate result of this fact—that double crostics are relatively uncomplicated to construct—is that they are not in great commercial demand. The two most prominent homes for double crostics—the Sunday *Times* and *Harper's*—are the autocratic province of one constructor—Thomas Middleton. Like crossword puzzles, though, double crostics are well worth constructing for less glamorous markets: a school, office, or organization publication; or just as a gift. I once heard of a correspondence that was carried on exclusively in double crostics, which struck me not only as classy but convenient; the solvers could presumably play around with their quotations if the puzzle wasn't working out quite right.

Choosing an appropriate message is the first step in constructing a double crostic. You may choose to emulate Mrs. Kingsley and edify your solver on the side, or, if you have a particular solver in mind, you may want to pick a quotation with special inside significance.

At any rate, there is one important restriction on the quotation you pick: *it must contain all the letters of the author and title of the work it comes from.* In the final puzzle, the first letters of the answers to the definitions will spell out this information.

This is the only inviolable rule about double crostic construction. In addition, Thomas Middleton has offered these two guidelines for standard double crostics. You may, of course, choose to modify them or just ignore them, depending on the leniency of the puzzle editor or puzzle fan for whom you are constructing:

- The quotation should be between 170 and 260 letters long.
- The number of clues should be between twenty-one and twenty-eight. In other words, there should be between twenty-one and twenty-eight letters in the author and the title of the work.

Remember that you can always edit the quotation to suit your needs; leaving out phrases and even prudently altering them are both legitimate. The author and title are also pliable: You can leave out a portion of the title, and you can drop the author's first name or just use the initial.

Once you have a suitable quotation, here's how to proceed: On a sheet of lined paper, write out the alphabet in a column, one letter to a line. Now, pigeonhole each letter of the quotation, from beginning to end, in its appropriate line. When you've reached the last letter—when all the letters of the quotation are organized in alphabetical order—cross off one of each letter (the letters you originally wrote down to label the lines). You now have a master list of all the letters in the double crostic.

To be really safe, you should go through this sorting process twice and make sure you haven't left out a letter—an easy mistake to make and one that will completely louse you up once you reach the end of the puzzle only to discover the errant letter. As a final check, count the number of letters on the master list to see that it checks with the number of letters in the quotation.

Next, take another sheet of paper and write down, in a column, the author and title of your quotation. This will be your answer list, containing the answers to the definitions. As you write these letters down, cross them off on the master list.

Now you're set for the nitty-gritty work of constructing double crostics: fitting the remaining letters on the master list into words that begin with the letters on the answers list. As you juggle the letters around, keep these strategies in mind:

- Before you start, and regularly thereafter, count up the number of available letters on the master list and divide it by the number of available initials on the answer list. This will give you the average length of each remaining answer. If at all possible, stay ahead of this figure—find answers that use up more letters than the average. When you get down to just a few answers left to form, your task will be simpler if you have the smallest possible number of letters to maneuver.

- Try to make compound words and words with suffixes. This will make it easier to juggle around letters from answer to answer. When you're trying to fit the last few letters into answers, it will be extremely useful to be able to steal a few letters from the end of another answer.

- Get rid of H's, F's, and W's. These three letters are the crostic constructor's migraines and you'll be stuck with many more than you can use if you don't plan ahead. So start picking them off in the first few answers you fill in, while you have lots of other letters to play with.

- This is another Middleton guideline, and again, you can modify it to suit your own standards: No two letters of any word of the quotation should appear in a single answer.

When your answer list is complete, and all the letters from the master list have been crossed off, the real work of the crostic's construction will be done. Two more steps remain: The first is to define each word on the word list.

The next and final step is the menial work of preparing the diagram. This entails arranging the quotation in a rectangular grid, with one black square at the end of each word. (There will probably have to be a few extra black squares at the end of the last word, to make the quotation fit into an even rectangle.) Number each square, and label each definition with a letter. Then, go through each answer letter by letter and under each letter, write the number of the square in the quotation that contains the same letter. At the same time, write the label-letter of the definition in the square of the quotation.

When you're finished, every letter on the answer list should have a number, to indicate the square of the quotation to which the solver should transfer it. Similarly, every square of the quotation should have a letter, to indicate the answer in which it appears.

One last word about constructing double crostics: If anyone should ever tell you that it's a waste of your time, should perhaps call it "futile"; if anyone has the nerve to ask you, "What is the goal?" recall Tennyson's words:

"To strive, to seek, to find, and not to yield."

Here are three double crostics that Thomas Middleton, the nation's leading constructor, recommends as typical of the genre. The third, you'll notice, employs cryptic clues.

		1 S	2 A	3 E		4 I	5 F	6 S	7 B	8 J
9 M	10 L	11 R	12 V	13 G		14 D	15 S	16 V	17 K		18 A
19 L	20 T		21 H	22 G	23 T	24 J	25 M	26 W		27 E	28 D
29 Q	30 I	31 C	32 B		33 X	34 L	35 M		36 I	37 V	38 E
	39 A	40 S	41 B	42 F	43 W	44 L		45 U		46 P	47 J
48 Q	49 N	50 X	51 G		52 X	53 I	54 A		55 Q		56 R
57 G	58 N	59 V	60 T	61 I	62 P	63 D	64 C	65 K		66 X	67 P
	68 K	69 J	70 T	71 B	72 Q		73 G	74 I	75 L	76 H	77 M
78 S	79 A	80 C	81 V		82 M	83 A	84 J	85 F	86 T	87 U	88 H
89 I	90 L		91 O	92 Q	93 K	94 X	95 C	96 A	97 M	98 J	99 I
100 L	101 H	102 P	103 S	104 R		105 M	106 S	107 D		108 U	109 K
110 E	111 S	112 V	113 C	114 G	115 Q	116 N		117 H	118 J	119 F	120 W
121 R	122 B		123 K	124 C	125 P	126 J	127 V	128 T	129 X	130 O	131 W
132 N	133 U		134 E	135 F	136 Q	137 H	138 K	139 O	140 V	141 J	142 M
	143 U	144 G		145 Q	146 L	147 X		148 O	149 U	150 H	151 K
152 R	153 D		154 U	155 N	156 M	157 I		158 V	159 O		160 S
	161 G	162 T	163 B		164 J	165 V	166 O	167 D	168 E		169 V
170 G	171 B	172 H	173 F	174 L		175 W		176 B	177 G	178 X	179 O
	180 W		181 C	182 D	183 X		184 K	185 I	186 W	187 O	188 F
	189 U	190 H	191 N	192 R	193 A		194 F	195 X		

	CLUES	WORDS

CLUES **WORDS**

A Cap. of the Sudan. . . . .
$\overline{193}\ \overline{2}\ \overline{18}\ \overline{39}\ \overline{54}\ \overline{79}\ \overline{83}\ \overline{96}$

B Parts of a country surrounded by the territory of another country .
$\overline{122}\ \overline{163}\ \overline{176}\ \overline{32}\ \overline{41}\ \overline{171}\ \overline{7}\ \overline{71}$

C 1928 Romberg operetta (2 wds. after *The*) . . . .
$\overline{80}\ \overline{95}\ \overline{113}\ \overline{181}\ \overline{31}\ \overline{64}\ \overline{124}$

D Soft and limp . . . .
$\overline{153}\ \overline{167}\ \overline{182}\ \overline{14}\ \overline{28}\ \overline{63}\ \overline{107}$

E Most peculiar . . . .
$\overline{110}\ \overline{134}\ \overline{168}\ \overline{3}\ \overline{27}\ \overline{38}$

F Treated as a celebrity . . . .
$\overline{42}\ \overline{85}\ \overline{5}\ \overline{173}\ \overline{194}\ \overline{119}\ \overline{135}\ \overline{188}$

G Power of moving from place to place . . . .
$\overline{51}\ \overline{57}\ \overline{73}\ \overline{114}\ \overline{161}\ \overline{177}\ \overline{13}\ \overline{22}\ \overline{144}\ \overline{170}$

H Derived from experience. . . . . .
$\overline{172}\ \overline{76}\ \overline{117}\ \overline{137}\ \overline{190}\ \overline{101}\ \overline{21}\ \overline{88}\ \overline{150}$

I Treating of in passing (2 wds.). . .
$\overline{157}\ \overline{185}\ \overline{53}\ \overline{61}\ \overline{74}\ \overline{99}\ \overline{36}\ \overline{4}\ \overline{30}\ \overline{89}$

J "All equal are within ___ gate" (2 wds.; Herbert, "The Temple") .
$\overline{98}\ \overline{126}\ \overline{141}\ \overline{164}\ \overline{24}\ \overline{118}\ \overline{8}\ \overline{47}\ \overline{69}\ \overline{84}$

K Peculiar. . . . .
$\overline{123}\ \overline{138}\ \overline{184}\ \overline{17}\ \overline{65}\ \overline{93}\ \overline{109}\ \overline{151}\ \overline{68}$

L Competitor for the America's Cup
$\overline{44}\ \overline{75}\ \overline{100}\ \overline{146}\ \overline{174}\ \overline{90}\ \overline{10}\ \overline{34}\ \overline{19}$

M Filled pastry turnovers (Lat. Am. cooking) . . . .
$\overline{25}\ \overline{82}\ \overline{77}\ \overline{97}\ \overline{9}\ \overline{105}\ \overline{142}\ \overline{156}\ \overline{35}$

N Back-number (2 wds.) . . . .
$\overline{49}\ \overline{58}\ \overline{116}\ \overline{155}\ \overline{191}\ \overline{132}$

O Torch for use in night processions
$\overline{159}\ \overline{187}\ \overline{130}\ \overline{91}\ \overline{148}\ \overline{179}\ \overline{139}\ \overline{166}$

P Robert Alphonso and William Howard, for instance. . . . .
$\overline{62}\ \overline{102}\ \overline{67}\ \overline{125}\ \overline{46}$

Q Construction workers, for instance (comp.). . . . .
$\overline{48}\ \overline{92}\ \overline{115}\ \overline{136}\ \overline{29}\ \overline{55}\ \overline{145}\ \overline{72}$

R Australian winner, Nobel Prize for Medicine, 1963 . . . .
$\overline{152}\ \overline{192}\ \overline{56}\ \overline{121}\ \overline{11}\ \overline{104}$

S Richard Wright novel (2 wds.). . .
$\overline{103}\ \overline{160}\ \overline{1}\ \overline{78}\ \overline{6}\ \overline{40}\ \overline{111}\ \overline{15}\ \overline{106}$

T Slipped away . . . .
$\overline{60}\ \overline{128}\ \overline{86}\ \overline{162}\ \overline{23}\ \overline{70}\ \overline{20}$

U Rapturous . . . .
$\overline{149}\ \overline{108}\ \overline{133}\ \overline{143}\ \overline{45}\ \overline{154}\ \overline{87}\ \overline{189}$

V Termination; decay; breaking up .
$\overline{16}\ \overline{169}\ \overline{112}\ \overline{81}\ \overline{37}\ \overline{59}\ \overline{127}\ \overline{140}\ \overline{158}\ \overline{165}\ \overline{12}$

W Brother of Mary and Martha (John 11:1–44) . . . .
$\overline{43}\ \overline{175}\ \overline{120}\ \overline{180}\ \overline{26}\ \overline{186}\ \overline{131}$

X Great Am. actor (1833–93; full name). . . . .
$\overline{147}\ \overline{178}\ \overline{33}\ \overline{129}\ \overline{183}\ \overline{52}\ \overline{50}\ \overline{66}\ \overline{195}\ \overline{94}$

Puzzle 25

				1 W	2 J	3 L	4 N		5 B	6 Q
7 H	8 C		9 J	10 F	11 S		12 Q	13 M	14 P	15 F	16 J
	17 U	18 H	19 J	20 L		21 M	22 P		23 F	24 J	25 U
	26 R	27 C	28 N	29 O	30 L	31 J		32 W	33 K	34 P	35 J
36 D		37 W		38 G	39 K	40 H	41 T		42 I	43 R	44 U
45 G	46 W	47 D	48 X		49 H	50 O	51 C		52 A	53 P	54 M
55 B	56 T	57 F	58 S	59 V	60 K		61 W	62 S	63 G	64 N	65 J
	66 H	67 E	68 B	69 X	70 G		71 Q	72 K	73 O		74 I
75 T	76 G	77 M	78 U	79 A	80 J	81 X		82 C	83 T		84 D
85 Q	86 G		87 M	88 O	89 S	90 L		91 A	92 T	93 K	
94 M	95 S	96 U	97 L		98 P	99 C	100 K	101 R	102 B	103 A	104 F
105 O	106 G		107 I	108 U		109 N	110 X		111 D	112 A	113 Q
	114 M	115 N	116 I	117 F	118 G	119 S	120 U		121 G	122 N	123 X
	124 O	125 D	126 T	127 B	128 P	129 X		130 I	131 P	132 G	133 U
134 S	135 D	136 V		137 K	138 Q	139 U		140 B	141 X	142 W	
143 P	144 W	145 D	146 G		147 E	148 N		149 G	150 H	151 C	152 R
	153 R	154 F	155 K	156 V		157 V	158 K	159 M	160 N	161 A	162 C
163 O	164 U	165 I	166 R		167 V	168 W		169 U	170 E	171 O	172 T
173 H	174 B	175 J	176 I	177 M	178 W		179 K	180 W	181 O		182 M
183 X	184 I	185 P	186 S	187 C	188 E	189 Q					

CLUES	WORDS

A Anc. Celtic stringed musical
instruments . . . .
52 79 91 103 112 161

B Prime Minister of Britain,
1908–16 . . . .
174 5 55 68 102 127 140

C Opposed by contrary proof . . . .
27 51 82 99 151 162 187 8

D This was originally a gondola race
in Venice. . . . .
135 145 36 47 84 111 125

E Mountain in Thessaly. . . . .
147 170 188 67

F "For the flesh ___ against the
Spirit" (Gal. 5:17) . . . .
117 154 15 23 57 104 10

G 1938 Gershwin song from "The
Goldwyn Follies" (3 wds.). . . . .
45 63 76 86 121 132 149 38 70 106 118 146

H Lightless, dark. . . . .
150 173 18 40 49 7 66

I Liberals, radicals (2 wds.) . . . . .
130 165 74 107 42 176 184 116

J "Mine enemies that trouble me
cast me ___" (3 wds.; Psalms 42,
"Book of Common Prayer"). . . .
19 35 175 2 16 31 65 80 9 24

K Open-sided sightseeing buses
(esp. Brit.) . . . .
158 33 179 60 72 100 137 39 155 93

L City in the Ruhr valley . . . .
3 20 30 90 97

M TV camera tube invented in 1923
by V. K. Zworykin . . . .
21 159 177 54 77 94 182 13 87 114

N Electric ray . . . .
115 160 4 109 148 28 64 122

O Bertie Wooster's creator . . . . . .
124 163 181 29 50 88 171 73 105

P Funeral ceremonies. . . . .
53 143 98 128 185 14 34 131 22

Q School subject that involves set
theory (2 wds.) . . . .
138 113 71 12 6 189 85

R Faded. . . . .
26 43 101 153 152 166

S Long, perforated, cylindrical
blocks used to tighten ropes supporting shipboard awnings, tents,
etc. . . . .
11 186 89 62 58 95 134 119

T Easily won, as a contest . . . . . .
172 56 126 75 41 92 83

U Vociferous. . . . .
44 108 78 133 164 96 169 17 120 25 139

V Mount on the easternmost prong
of the peninsula of Chalcidice,
Greece . . . .
157 167 156 59 136

W Throughout the entire country . .
178 1 32 46 168 180 61 37 142 144

X "Then is ___ near," says Hamlet
on being told, "The world's grown
honest". . . . .
129 123 183 48 69 81 141 110

Puzzle 26

	1 Y	2 F	3 B	4 E	5 V		6 G	7 T	8 Q	9 W
10 J		11 S	12 V	13 U	14 K	15 Y	16 C	17 W	18 A	19 D	20 G
21 T		22 O	23 C	24 M	25 Q	26 V		27 K	28 B	29 G
30 E	31 D	32 F	33 T		34 L	35 U		36 V		37 Q	38 A
39 B	40 J	41 Y	42 R	43 D	44 E		45 V	46 Y	47 I	48 G	49 W
50 X		51 D	52 J	53 T	54 Y		55 O	56 U		57 V
58 B	59 N	60 F	61 P	62 X	63 G		64 F	65 B	66 I	67 S	68 Y
69 E		70 X	71 R		72 Y		73 M	74 T	75 R	76 N	77 I
78 H		79 S	80 V	81 J	82 P	83 E	84 B	85 A		86 V	87 G
	88 T	89 M	90 H	91 S	92 F	93 N	94 Z		95 N	96 S	97 Y
	98 P	99 M	100 A	101 V		102 G	103 C	104 Q	105 F	106 D	107 E
108 U	109 Z		110 W	111 A	112 O		113 N	114 R	115 X	116 J
117 D	118 V		119 M	120 U		121 Y	122 F	123 C	124 E		125 G
126 W	127 H		128 C	129 V	130 K	131 J	132 F		133 I	134 Z
135 X		136 V	137 C	138 N	139 H	140 K		141 J	142 D	143 Q	144 M
145 A	146 T	147 O		148 X	149 E	150 H		151 U	152 R	153 S	154 O
155 Z	156 C	157 K		158 J	159 L		160 W	161 H	162 S	163 I	164 X
165 L	166 D	167 F		168 H	169 C	170 M	171 G	172 R	173 D	174 J
175 O	176 I	177 Z		178 W	179 L	180 H	181 J	182 A

CLUES

A "___ trouble" might be a wounded wooden soldier heard in "Macbeth" . . . .

B Poet from Ludlow. All erotic verses! . . . .

C Call a hog out of the wood. . . . .

D Greek girl heaping two Roman wrecks . . . .

E Doggone! The underworld is a small space! . . . .

F Upstart grows fat, ungainly, in contests (3 wds.) . . . .

G One balmy hour briefly made sweet (2 wds.). . . . .

H Mexican town back in a Dane's neighboring county . . . .

I Spanish town in Guatemala gains tourism. . . . .

J She has a gown torn to shreds, between you and an adult male (2 wds.) . . . .

K Sleeping accommodation in the way of a writer . . . .

L President Grant, after all, needs him . . . .

M Name three extremes, let in chaos

N Tricky barb; it might be a garden pest. . . . .

O Sound to do with sensitivity? . . .

P Little Giant of old from Rotterdam . . . .

Q Indian chief who gives lots of cash to an international group. . . . . .

R Small street with badly lit interiors give a heightened effect .

S Conceited cutups playing with knothead. . . . .

T Alarm Scots in turmoil . . . .

U Tear to shreds in turn. . . . .

V "'Bare Teeth," by a riotous Irish company (2 wds.). . . . .

W Clues core unclues, possibly . . . .

X Giant of old who had an oil spill in his home town . . . .

Y River flowing pure as the elements . . . .

Z Little turnover at first of year . . .

WORDS

A 18 38 85 100 111 145 182

B 3 28 39 58 65 84

C 103 123 128 137 156 169 16 23

D 31 51 106 117 142 166 173 19 43

E 69 83 107 124 149 4 30 44

F 60 92 105 132 2 32 64 122 167

G 171 20 29 63 87 102 125 6 48

H 78 90 139 150 168 180 127 161

I 47 66 77 133 163 176

J 10 40 52 81 174 116 158 131 141 181

K 14 27 130 140 157

L 165 34 159 179

M 24 99 119 144 170 73 89

N 93 138 95 113 59 76

O 55 112 147 154 175 22

P 98 61 82

Q 104 8 37 143 25

R 42 75 172 114 71 152

S 153 91 162 79 67 96 11

T 33 7 88 53 74 21 146

U 13 120 35 151 56 108

V 57 136 86 12 101 118 45 80 36 129 5 26

W 126 17 110 160 9 49 178

X 50 115 62 70 135 148 164

Y 15 46 1 54 121 72 97 68 41

Z 109 155 177 134 94

5
after
crossword
puzzles

When a felon's not engaged in his employment
Or maturing his felonious little plans,
His capacity for innocent enjoyment,
Is just as great as any honest man's.

W. S. Gilbert *The Pirates of Penzance*

This chapter is for the crossword addict who has run out of crosswords, who has lost his crosswords, who has left his crosswords home, who is driving a motor vehicle and would endanger lives if he started working on a crossword, or who has just plain had enough of crosswords for a while. There is innocent enjoyment to be derived elsewhere, and this is it: These are the three best noncrossword games I know. All of them are sure to appeal to crossword fans, and all three can be played in any circumstances, with no more equipment than a pencil and paper.

This chapter also includes three variations on the best commercial crossword substitute available—Scrabble.

SUPER GHOST

Super Ghost is the old game of Ghost with one ingenious, elevating twist. Like its simpler ancestor, Super Ghost begins with one player calling out a letter. The player to the starter's left adds a second letter, the third player tacks on a third letter, and so on, around and around the circle of players, the string of letters growing longer with every move. A player loses the round when the letter he adds turns the string into a complete word.

Here is the twist: In Ghost, players can only add letters to the end of the string. In Super Ghost, a player can add a letter to the beginning of the string or the end.

The other rules of Super Ghost are identical to those of Ghost. You must have a word in mind every time you add a letter. After any move you make, another player can challenge you to reveal the word you are forming. If there is no word and you were bluffing, you lose the round; if you weren't, the challenger loses the round.

When you lose a round, you get a letter—first G, then H, O, S, and T. After you lose five rounds and your score spells out a complete word, you are out of the game.

You don't lose a round if you form a proper noun or a word of three letters or less. (Similarly, you can't answer a challenge with a proper noun.)

Here's how a game of Super Ghost with four players might go.

> Alice: L
> Brian: LA
> Charlotte: LAK

Now in Ghost, the fourth player—let's call him Danny— would be in a pretty tight spot. He could challenge Charlotte, who would probably laugh, or he could say *E* and add a letter to his score. In Super Ghost, he has this move to make:

> Danny: FLAK

Alice would be up the creek now in old Ghost. Not in Super Ghost.

Alice: WFLAK

Brian cannot think of any word that includes the letters WFLAK, and so he challenges Alice. Alice reveals her word—SNOWFLAKE—and Brian adds a letter to his score.

As practice for Super Ghost, see if you can find words in which the following groups of letters appear:

SSW	YNON	EBU	UNKA
UEU	CIF	REEM	OSAI
GHTH	XTB	LYTHE	DAGE
CKGR	EMSE	CHB	NORG

Answers are on page 147.

THE LICENSE PLATE GAME

I learned this game from Will Shortz, one of the nation's top puzzle editors and the only person in the world with a college degree in crossword puzzles—a B.A. in Enigmatology from the University of Indiana.

The license plate game is an easy way to make a long car ride interesting, particularly if you're driving alone or with stodgy company and can't launch into a group game like Super Ghost. The object of the game is simple: to think of a word that uses—in order, but not necessarily consecutively—the letters of a license plate you spot. Short words are classier, and classiest of all is a word that begins with the first letter of the license plate and ends with the plate's last letter. You can use these criteria to work out a system of keeping score, or you can just play one plate at a time.

For instance, suppose you drive by this license plate: CIH 434. One good solution is DECIPHER—the C, I, and H appear in their order on the plate. Even better is simply CIPHER. And best of all is CINCH, which is as short as you'll get with CIH, and has the added cachet of beginning with C and ending with the H.

Certain tendencies in the manufacture of license plates work against the license plate game. Vanity plates usually spoil the game by doing all the work for you. DISPEL is about as good as you'll do outside the United Nations building, and M.D. plates will only leave you stuck in the mud. Nevertheless, enough cars still carry meaningless combinations of letters to keep the game exciting. See how you fare with these sample license plates (not all of these have perfect solutions that begin with the first letter and end with the last):

VYL	IBC	SDM
III	RBI	QZL
YWY	VLO	QEY
LLC	WOW	MBA
CUY	CCO	AII

Answers are on page 147.

RADAR

The name of this game comes from the fact that in almost every round, the word RADAR has a way of popping up. So do the words TEETH, SEXES, and LLAMA. More about this later.

Radar is a game for two: One thinks up a five-letter word and the other tries to guess it. The guesser goes about his task by proposing five-letter words to the thinker. For each word proposed, the thinker responds by telling *how many letters in the proposed word appear in the mystery word.*

For example, suppose the mystery word is PRAWN, and the guesser proposes the word BREAK. The thinker will answer "two" because two of the letters of BREAK appear in PRAWN.

An important note: If the guesser proposes a word that repeats letters, the thinker should count each repeated letter separately. For instance, if the mystery word is PRAWN and the guesser proposes PAPER, the thinker will reply "four" because four of the letters in PAPER—the first P, the A, and the second P, and the R—appear in PRAWN.

The best way for you to proceed as a guesser is to keep a list of every word you propose and its results. In one corner, write out an alphabet and cross out letters as you eliminate them, and circle letters as you determine them.

The ideal answer for a guesser, short of hitting a perfect five, is zero—all the letters in the proposed word get conveniently crossed out. By methodically chipping your way through the alphabet, proposing words with felicitous combinations of letters, you'll eventually pin down the mystery word.

Here is the significance of the game's name. Consider what happens if you propose a word that has five different letters and the answer is "one." You're still floundering: You have no letters to circle and no letters to eliminate. But if you propose RADAR—or TEETH, SEXES, LLAMA, or any other word that contains two pairs of different letters—any answer you get will give you a definite piece of information. Take RADAR:

> *If the answer is 0:* You're in great shape. You cross off all three letters from your alphabet and move on to the next word.
>
> *If the answer is 1:* The letter could only be D. The R and the A come in pairs; if the mystery word contained either of these, the thinker would have to answer "two."
>
> *If the answer is 2:* You know the two refers to the pair of R's or the pair of A's. In other words, you've got a letter of the mystery word narrowed down to two possibilities and you can eliminate the D.
>
> *If the answer is 3:* This could only refer to one of the pairs plus the D. So circle the D and note that one more letter of the mystery word is either the R or the A.
>
> *If the answer is 4:* Circle the R and the A and cross off the D.
>
> *If the answer is 5:* Life is easy.

Here are a few variations of Radar

For competitors: Both players think up a word and see who discovers the other's in the fewest guesses.

For families: An unlimited number of players compete as guessers, taking turns proposing words, and keeping track of the information the other players' guesses reveal. The player who figures out the word first, wins.

For jugglers: Play with six letters, or seven, if you dare. I've never heard of a game of Radar with eight or more letters, but give it a try—you'll make history.

For hot-shots: Guess the mystery word without using pencil and paper.

THREE VARIATIONS ON SCRABBLE

These three versions can be played singly, or in combination with each other.

Wall Street Scrabble

When a player's turn comes around, before he sets out a word, he can trade any letter from his rack for a letter on the board *as long as the new letter on the board forms a legitimate word.* The player may then use the newly acquired letter or letters at full value to form his own word.

In a more conservative version of this rule, a player can only trade for a blank (if he replaces it with the letter it represents on the board). The player can then use the blank as a wild card for his own purposes.

Backscrabbble

If a player's word also forms a word reading backwards, he gets full credit for both words—double credit, in other words.

A more radical version of this rule permits players to set out a word in reverse even if it does not also form a word reading forward. Of course if a word does make sense backward and forward the player gets double credit.

Grabble

This variation works best late at night with a lot of players. All the letters are laid out face up next to the board. At an agreed upon signal, all the players grab for the seven letters of their choice. After this has been done, and all the pieces that fell to the floor have been picked up, the game begins, *with the letters still face up.* When it comes time for a player to pick new letters, he scans the remaining choices and selects the letters he likes best. In addition to reducing Scrabble to a game of pure skill, this is a good version for players who have lost the little racks from their scrabble sets.

WORKSHEET ANSWERS

DOUBLE DEFINITION
1. CLUBS
2. GRAVE
3. CARDINAL
4. GROUND
5. EXPRESS

HIDDEN WORDS
1. BINGE
2. BANANA
3. MYTH
4. INTIMATE
5. MONGREL

HOMOPHONES
1. MAINE
2. BAND
3. WHACKS
4. RUSSELL
5. ABOMINABLE

REVERSALS
1. POT
2. RATS or STAR
3. MOOD
4. REPAID
5. DEIFIED

WORD CHAINS
1. THINKING
2. MISTRUST
3. THEIRS
4. ANAPEST
5. TWINED

CONTAINERS
1. ASH-AM-ED
2. THE-ORE-M
3. CH-AS-E
4. BI-SO-N
5. MA-I-N

FRAGMENTS
1. (S)TABLE
2. PRINCES(S)
3. CA(RPE)T
4. TRI(BUN)AL
5. CAME(O)

ANAGRAMS
1. PLEATS
2. CRASS
3. MATE
4. HAMLET
5. DEMOCRAT

COMBINATIONS
1. H-IND-ER (container, hidden word)
2. CROS-SWORDS (wordchain, anagram)
3. DOONES-BURY (wordchain: homophone, anagram)
4. A-CHILL-ES (container, reversal)
5. PSYCHO-ANAL-Y-SIS (container, wordchain, fragment)

ANSWERS TO EXAMPLES
IN CHAPTER 5

You may discover other answers; here are the ones I had in mind:

Super Ghost

CROSSWORD
QUEUE
EIGHTH
BACKGROUND
SYNONYM
FANCIFUL
TEXTBOOK
THEMSELVES
REBUKE
PREEMINENT
POLYTHEISM
MATCHBOX
DRUNKARD
PROSAIC
ADAGE
INORGANIC

The License Plate Game

VINYL
BIKINI
BYWAY
LILAC
COUNTY
IAMBIC
RABBI
VOLCANO
WALLOW
CALICO
SODIUM
QUIZZICAL
QUERY
RUMBA
ALIBI

the answers

Puzzle 1

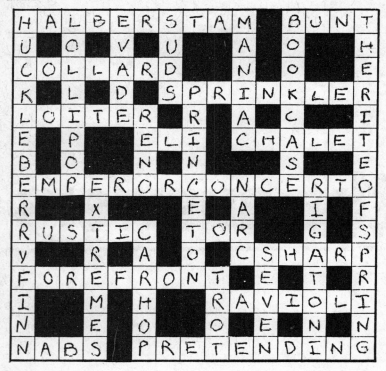

NOTES (breakdowns of the subsidiary definitions that are not self-explanatory)

ACROSS

1. HAL-BERSTAM
6. B(L)UNT
8. ("collared")
9. SP-RINK-LE(A)R
11. (EXP)LOITER
13. (R)ELI(C)
14. CHA-LE-T
15. EMPEROR-CONCERT-O
19. RUST-IC
22. C-SH-ARP
28. PRE-TENDING

DOWN

1. HUCKLEBERRY-FINN
2. LO-LLIP-OP
3. EV-AD-E
4. S(P)UDS
5. MA-NIAC
7. THE RITE ["the right"] OF(F)SPRING
10. PRINCE-TON
17. N-ARC
18. RIGA-TONI

Puzzle 2

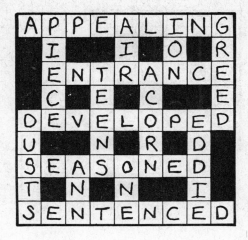

Puzzle 3

Puzzle 4

Puzzle 5

Puzzle 6

Puzzle 7

Puzzle 8

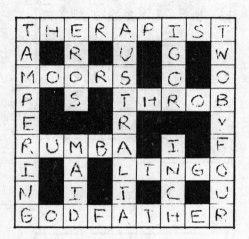

NOTES:

DOWN:

3. AUSTR-AL-IA
4. (R)IGOR
10. INCH(OATE)

Puzzle 9

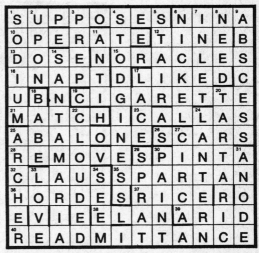

Theme Words are Nina, Pinta, *and* Santa Maria. Nina*'s Variations are* nickel *and* sodium, *corresponding to its component parts* Ni *and* Na; Pinta*'s Variations are* inapt *and* paint, *anagrams;* Santa Maria*'s Variations are* Claus *and* Callas, *names associated with* Santa *and* Maria.

Across. 1. SUP(POSE)S 10. OP(ERA)TE (*poet* anag.) 12. TIN-E 13. DOSE (homophone of *dos*) 15. (c)ORACLES 17. L(IKE)D 19. C-IGARETTE (anag. +*c*) 21. MATCH (double def.) 25. AB-ALONE 26. SCARS (anag.) 28. R(EM)OVE 35. SP(ART)AN 36. HORDE (anag.) 37. R-ICE 38. ELAN (hidden) 39. A-RID 40. READMITTANCE (anag.) *Down.* 2. (co)UPON 3. P(R)EP 4. STODGINESS (anag.) 5. ST(A)IR 7. IN-LET 8. NEE-D 9. ABSC-(m)ESS(y) (*scab* anag.) 11. ANTI (hidden) 17. L-ACE 18. B-ABE 20. TAR-TAR-I-C 22. CLOUDED (anag.) 24. L-(AN)TERN 25. ARCHER (pun) 27. CI-RCA (*car* anag.) 29. SPRAT (*tarps* rev.) 31. AN-ODE 33. LOVE (pun) 34. SEEM (homophone of *seam*)

Puzzle 10

Across. 1. DOUBLE T 6. DER-BY (*red* rev.) 10. EMBAL-M (anag. + *m*) 12. RO-YALS (rev.) 13. DANE (homophone) 14. BIF-OCAL (*fib* rev. + *cola* anag.) 15. P AND A 16. R AFTER S 18. (m)ORGAN (pun) 19. AN EM ON E 21. TWIN E 22. DO-ZEN 24. CITADEL (anag.) 26. STAYS (double def.) 27. (nightin)GALE 30. N ONCE 32. VEE R 33. RI(b)-SORIAL (*sailor* anag.) 35. ECRU (anag.) 37. REPRI-EVE (*riper* anag.) 38. R(UP-E)E 39. GUESSES (hidden) 40. S TILTED 41. STUDS (double def.) *Down.* 1. D E SPOT 2. U-BANG-I 3. B AND AN A 4. EM BRACE 5. TRIANGLE (anag.) 6. D OFF ED 7. EYOT (hidden) 8. RACE (double def.) 9. B-LARNEY (anag. + *b*) 11. LEA-NED (*den* rev.) 13. DAR(row)-WIN 17. SEN SE-LESS 20. M(O-TOR)IST (pun) 23. ZANIES (anag.) 24. C OVER S 25. TWE(et)-(chi)RP 26. S(N)ORES 27. GRUE-L (anag. + *l*) 28. ARRET (rev.) 29. LI(EG)E 31. C(AVE)D 34. SPUD (hidden) 36. CUT(e)

Puzzle 11

	1	2	3	4	5	6	7	8	9	10	11	12	13	14	15
A	I	N	T	H	E	M	A	N	G	R	O	V	E	S	W
B	A	M	P	S	W	H	E	R	E	T	H	E	P	Y	T
C	H	O	N	R	O	M	P	S	T	H	E	R	E	I	S
D	P	E	A	C	E	F	R	O	M	T	W	E	L	V	E
E	T	I	L	L	T	W	O	E	V	E	N	C	A	R	I
F	B	O	U	S	L	I	E	A	R	O	U	N	D	A	N
G	D	S	N	O	O	Z	E	F	O	R	T	H	E	R	E
H	S	N	O	T	H	I	N	G	E	L	S	E	T	O	D
I	O	I	N	B	E	N	G	A	L	T	O	M	O	V	E
J	A	T	A	L	L	I	S	S	E	L	D	O	M	I	F
K	E	V	E	R	D	O	N	E	B	U	T	M	A	D	D
L	O	G	S	A	N	D	E	N	G	L	I	S	H	M	E
M	N	G	O	O	U	T	I	N	T	H	E	M	I	D	D
N	A	Y	S	U	N	N	O	E	L	C	O	W	A	R	D

1. STABLE (double def.) 2. EPOCHS (anag.) 3. AVOWAL (homophone) 4. SER-APHIM (anag.) 5. O(VI)NE ("1" divided by "6") 6. NO(V)EL 7. SHAMBLES (double def.) 8. GENESIS (anag.) 9. R(OUT)ING 10. END-OW 11. EVEN (double def.) 12. TENDER (double def.) 13. IN-DO-LENT 14. NO(r)SE 15. G-ADDED 16. S(NOW)ING 17. THROW (anag.) 18. OO(M)PH (anag. + *m*) 19. AME(TH[e])YST (*steamy* anag.) 20. LOG-O 21. LOCUS-T 22. FLOUNDER (double def.) 23. (d)ROUGH(t) 24. OFF-END 25. MATE (anag.) 26. THE-ME (pun) 27. HOOD (double def.) 28. ELDER (double def.) 29. A-ERIE 30. TWIST (hidden) 31. LI(MI)T 32. AND-ANTE 33. NORM-AN 34. TUMBLER (double def.) 35. IV(OR)Y 36. CAP-SIZE

Puzzle 12

←	I	L	L	I	A	M	T	→	L	L
A	↘	A	↓	↗	→	R	H	A	I	R
G	R	→	←	A	↙	A	T	I	O	O
I	T	D	↙	R	R	C	A	L	→	B
T	I	M	→	D	I	↓	C	U	↓	I
T	A	X	←	I	↘	←	K	A	T	→
A	R	R	O	←	A	T	T	A	C	H
R	O	A	↓	T	G	A	U	C	H	O
I	V	Y	T	R	O	T	R	T	←	O
U	↓	A	T	A	R	I	D	U	K	D
←	D	I	A	T	A	C	U	P	I	D

Puzzle 13

PER	S	EU	S	GOR	G	O	N
A	C	H	ILL	ES	HE	CTO	R
M	O	B	Y	DI	CK	AH	AB
BU	R	RHA	MI	L	T	O	N
LA	ER	TE	S	H	AM	L	ET
TOR	TO	I	S	E	H	A	RE
LI	N	COL	N	D	O	UGL	AS
ST	G	E	OR	GED	RA	G	ON
MON	I	TOR	M	E	R	RIM	AC
TH	ESE	US	M	IN	OT	A	UR
ROO	SE	V	E	L	TWI	LL	KIE
D	AR	RO	W	B	R	Y	AN
S	CH	ME	L	ING	L	OU	IS

Puzzle 14

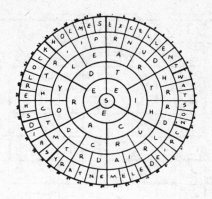

Puzzle 15

KR	KKт	KB	K	Q	QB	Qкт	QR
F	E	S	T	O	O	N	S
E	K	E	W	U	U	U	T
I	E	D	R	A	E	D	E
S	D	U	E	A	C	I	N
A	L	E	V	H	K	I	S
L	E	T	A	A	N	E	E
S	D	U	M	S	T	D	R
E	D	N	P	T	W	E	S
O	G	A	E	E	L	A	N
M	U	L	D	I	E	S	E
A	S	E	E	A	H	S	A
R	E	D	E	E	M	E	R

KR KKт QB K Q KB Qкт QR

Puzzle 16

F	R	E	N	C	H	D	R	E	S	S	I	N	G
R	E	P	R	O	O	F	E	X	P	A	N	S	E
E	P	I	C	M	O	T	H	E	R	L	I	T	N
E	E	T	A	M	D	O	E	S	U	E	T	F	T
P	L	A	T	E	A	U	A	D	C	H	I	L	I
A	S	P	E	N	S	T	R	I	E	S	A	L	L
I	C	H	A	T	P	A	S	S	B	E	T	T	E
N	A	T	C	H	9	R	A	S	B	R	E	A	D
P	L	A	T	E	O	B	L	U	E	V	S	L	I
A	I	R	S	A	H	O	W	A	D	I	N	E	R
R	C	M	E	R	E	R	E	D	O	L	E	N	T
F	O	R	E	T	A	S	T	E	R	E	T	R	Y

The nine unclued lights each referred to another light in the diagram. Each of these, when given 1 Across—FRENCH DRESSING—was to be considered as a French word, rather than as its clued English meaning, and the English translation of that word entered. Thus 15A referred to 47A, which was MERE; the French word MERE was then put into English at 15A: MOTHER.

ACROSS

11. rep(reversal)-roof
12. ex-panse (homonym of "pants")
13. hidden
15. MOTHER(MERE)
17. lit(reversal)
19. two meanings
20. Tet(palindrome)
21. anagram
23. pun
24. as-pens
25. (the en)tries
27. ALL(TOUT)
28. c.-hat
30. two meanings

32. homonym
33. anagram
35. bras(h)
36. BREAD(PAIN)
38. PLATE(PLATEAU)
40. homonym
41. two meanings
43. HOW(COMMENT)
45. anagram
47. me-re
48. re(do)lent
49. anagram
50. re-(pan)try

DOWN

1. f(R)ee
2. repel-S.(reversal)
3. anagram
4. co(M-men)t
5. two meanings
6. re(hear-s.)al
7. two meanings
8. homonym
9. anagram
10. gent(l)le
14. CAT(CHAT)
16. t.-out
18. Tell tale
21. pain(ting)

22. anagram
26. anagram
28. c.(Ali)c.-O
29. (t)act
31. (h)arbors
34. anagram
35. bo(he)a
36. BED(LIT)
37. DIRTY(SALE)
38. par(reversal)
39. ARM(BRAS)
42. see(m)
44. hidden
46. two meanings

Puzzle 17

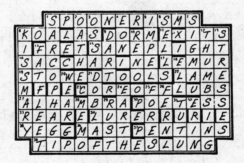

The title is a reference to the Reverend William Spooner.

ACROSS: 8. OK(rev.)-alas; 9. dorm(ouse); 11. anag.; 14. f(re)t.: 15. pun; 16. anag.; 17. l(emu)r; 19. to-a-D(loots-rev.)S; 22. 2 mngs.; 23. four of clubs; 27. a(L-ham)bra; 30. Poe(set-rev.)'s; 33. R.-ear; 34. anag.; 35. (da)y-egg; 36. homonym; 37. snip-net(rev.).

DOWN: 1 anag.; 2. anag.; 3. ass-o(rev.); 4. Noe(l), rev.; 5. "lie" anag. around "MP"; 6. homonym; 7. s(t)igma; 8. pun, Miss Carrie; 9. Dartmouth; 10. one-R. (rev.); 12. anag.; 13. s(electing)-tresses; 14. pun; 18. el-l; 20. wear(y); 21. bold(anag.)-a; 24. (t)ear-th(e); 25. fores(t); 26. fe-RN; 28. me-M.O.; 29. (t)rust; 31. pun; 32. hidden.

Puzzle 18

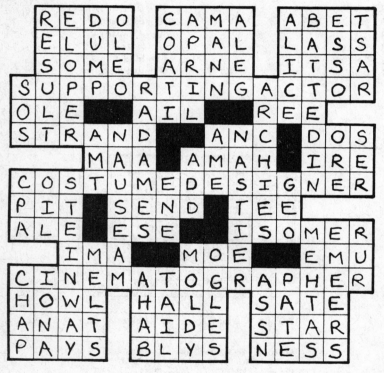

Puzzle 19

Puzzle 20

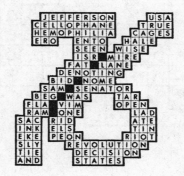

Puzzle 21

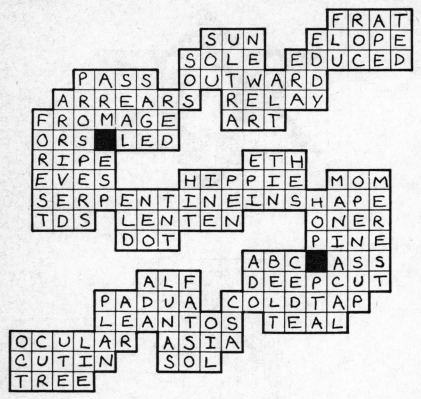

Puzzle 22

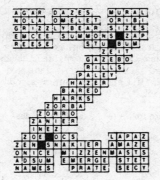

Puzzle 23

Puzzle 24

KEN FOLLETT: EYE OF THE NEEDLE

The Government Code and Cipher School . . . was not really a school but a collection of chess champions, musicians, mathematicians and crossword puzzle enthusiasts dedicated to the belief that if a man could invent a code a man could crack it.

A	Khartoum	M	Empanadas
B	Enclaves	N	Old hat
C	New Moon	O	Flambeau
D	Flaccid	P	Tafts
E	Oddest	Q	Hard-hats
F	Lionized	R	Eccles
G	Locomotion	S	Native Son
H	Empirical	T	Escaped
I	Touching on	U	Ecstatic
J	The church's	V	Dissolution
K	Eccentric	W	Lazarus
L	Yachtsman	X	Edwin Booth

Puzzle 25

(LEWIS) CARROLL: ALICE IN WONDERLAND

"Ahem!" said the Mouse. . . . "This is the driest thing I know . . . 'William the Conqueror, whose cause was favoured by the pope, was soon submitted to by the English, who wanted leaders, and had been of late much accustomed to usurpation and conquest.' "

A	Crwths	M	Iconoscope
B	Asquith	N	Numbfish
C	Rebutted	O	Wodehouse
D	Regatta	P	Obsequies
E	Ossa	Q	New math
F	Lusteth	R	Dimmed
G	Love Walked In	S	Euphroes
H	Aphotic	T	Runaway
I	Left wing	U	Loudmouthed
J	In the teeth	V	Athos
K	Charabancs	W	Nationwide
L	Essen	X	Doomsday

Puzzle 26

(MARK) TWAIN: THE MYSTERIOUS STRANGER

Power, money, . . . persecution—these can lift at a colossal humbug—push it a little—weaken it a little, century by century, but only laughter can blow it to rags and atoms at a blast. Against the assault of laughter nothing can stand.

A	Toyland	N	Rabbit
B	Waller	O	Intact
C	Agalloch	P	Ott
D	Iphigenia	Q	Uncas
E	Nutshell	R	Stilts
F	Tugs of war	S	Stuck-up
G	Honey lamb	T	Tocsins
H	Ensenada	U	Rotate
I	Malaga	V	Abbey Theatre
J	Young woman	W	Nucleus
K	Scott	X	Goliath
L	Taft	Y	Euphrates
M	Entitle	Z	Runty